W9-BAA-548

Nicole Wilde, CPDT-KA

Don't Leave Me!

Step-by-Step Help for Your Dog's Separation Anxiety

Don't Leave Me! Step-by-Step Help
for Your Dog's Separation Anxiety
by Nicole Wilde, CPDT-KA

Copyright ©2010 by Nicole Wilde

Published by:
Phantom Publishing
P.O. Box 2814
Santa Clarita, CA 91386
www.phantompub.com

First Edition

All rights reserved.
No part of this book may be used or reproduced in any manner whatsoever without written permission from the author, except for the inclusion of brief quotations in a review.

Library of Congress Control Number: 2010935907

ISBN 978-0-9817227-3-3

Photo credits:

p.1 Steven Robertson
p.23 Walik
p.35 Helen Hollander
p.63 Rodolfo Sadeugra
p.74 Kirk Pollard
p.79 John B. McClatchey, Jr.
p.102 Gary Bilek
p.107 Barbara Helgeson
p.128 Mychelle Blake

All other photos including cover photo and design by Nicole Wilde.

For Sierra

Other books by Nicole Wilde:

Living with Wolfdogs

Wolfdogs A-Z: Behavior, Training & More

So You Want to be a Dog Trainer

It's Not the Dogs, It's the People! A Dog Trainer's Guide to Training Humans

One on One: A Dog Trainer's Guide to Private Lessons

Help for Your Fearful Dog

Getting a Grip on Aggression Cases

Energy Healing for Dogs

The information and suggestions herein are not intended to take the place of professional treatment or advice by a licensed veterinarian or veterinary behaviorist.

The pronoun "he" is used throughout this book to refer to dogs. It implies no gender bias and is employed simply for ease of reading.

Acknowledgements

Valerie Pollard, good friend and trainer extraordinaire, thanks for all the time you spent on this project, and for the excellent suggestions and support. Your input was invaluable and improved the book immeasurably.

Mychelle Blake, thanks for reading the manuscript despite your crazy busy schedule, and for the helpful suggestions. You always make good points, and I still don't know how you get so much done in a day!

Suzanne Clothier, thank you for making me reconsider my original thinking on some important topics. I was on the fence, and thanks to you, am now firmly back on the side that is aligned with not only my mind, but my spirit.

Cathy Bruce, Amber Burckhalter, Helen Hollander, Victoria Stilwell, Casey Lomonaco, and Valerie Pollard, thank you all for sharing the stories of your clients' dogs, and in some cases, your own dogs. The narratives were interesting, funny, and downright scary at times, and I know your generosity will help many readers.

Laura Bourhenne, thanks for reviewing the protocol chapters even though you were busy studying for an exam, which you no doubt aced.

Janine Pierce, thanks for the helpful chats about protocols early on. Much appreciated!

Laurie Williams, thanks for the assistance on the Rally information.

To C.C., I've thanked you in all of my books and yet I feel I could never thank you enough. I'm eternally grateful for your love, support, and patience, not to mention your willingness to sort through all of the dog (and wolf) dilemmas over the years. You're the best.

And though I haven't yet taught her to read, I must give howls of thanks to Sierra, our fur-kid, cover girl, and catalyst for this book. Thank you for being such an excellent teacher, and for helping to heal my heart.

Table of Contents

Part III: Behavior Modification

Part IV: A Quartet of Cool Tools

Part V: The Light at the End of the Tunnel

Introduction

Dogs, like humans, are highly social creatures. They enjoy the company of others, forge strong emotional attachments, and live in communal groups. In modern society, we have become our dogs' packs—their families. This arrangement has many benefits for both dogs and humans, and affords the opportunity to form close bonds of love and trust. But just as some children become nervous when their parents are away, many dogs experience anxiety when their people are absent.

The level of stress a dog feels when isolated or when separated from a particular person or persons may be mild, moderate, or in some cases, so intense that it constitutes a state of full-blown panic. Dealing with this type of issue can cause owners to feel a measure of strain as well. As a loving dog owner, it can be both frustrating and heart-wrenching to know that your dog is suffering and yet to be unable to convey that you'll be returning shortly, or that being left alone is not the end of the world.

You may have read articles about separation anxiety, asked friends for advice, or even consulted with a professional dog trainer or behavior specialist. Perhaps the prescribed rehabilitation plans seemed reasonable, but implementing them was not feasible. Or maybe the information you received was confusing, as it conflicted with suggestions from other sources. Perhaps you've already tried a few techniques or attempted a lengthy behavioral protocol, only to give up in dismay.

Whether your current attempt to solve your dog's difficulties is the beginning of a new journey or another stop along what has seemed like an endless road, I have two pieces of good news: first, you are not in this alone. As a professional dog trainer who specializes in behavior issues, I have helped many of my clients and their dogs through separation-related problems. I have coached them each step of the way until their dogs could safely be left alone, whether for five minutes or five hours.

I am also a dog mom. When my husband and I finally decided to get another dog a year after our last dog had passed, I scoured the local shelters and humane societies. Three months of intense searching yielded our perfect match—a lovely, gentle, year-and-a-half old Siberian Husky-Keeshond mix. During the adoption process, the staff member who handled our paperwork revealed that the dog had been in the shelter four times previously. We soon found out why. Sierra, as we named her, not only had the talent of Houdini, but also had serious separation issues. It was easy to imagine her watching her owners leave, and then escaping in a frantic attempt to follow them.

During the first two weeks with our new girl, I would return home from doing errands to find her panting heavily, eyes wild. Although she hadn't destroyed anything, she'd clearly been upset. To gauge the intensity of her distress, I set up a camcorder and then left the house for 45 minutes. A review of the footage revealed Sierra whining while pacing from door to window, back and forth, scanning the area where she'd seen us leave. Her whining progressed to intermittent barking, which escalated into a frantic series of barks, and finally, a mournful, pitiful howling that tore at my heart.

As emotionally difficult as dealing with Sierra's rehabilitation process was at times, having dealt with separation issues both professionally and personally has placed me in the perfect position to support you through your own dog's healing process. You'll be hearing more about Sierra's journey throughout the book, as I will share the techniques that were effective in helping her.

The second bit of good news is that there are now better behavior protocols and a greater number of supplementary products available than ever before to address separation issues. You will find them described in these pages.

The length of time required for your dog to stop feeling anxious when left alone will depend on the severity of the issue, your dog's temperament, your home environment, and the amount of effort put forth. But know that in the majority of cases, the issue is solvable, or at least manageable.

If your dog's stress level is mild, vast improvements could be seen in as little as one to three weeks. In moderate cases, however, recovery can be more on the order of a few months or longer. In extreme cases, it could take many months or even upwards of a year, but even then, it would be realistic to expect to see some progress within the first few months. *The most valuable asset your dog will have throughout the rehabilitation process is you.* So as a caring owner who wants to help your beloved dog to feel secure and to have a good quality of life, take heart, have patience, and know that your goals are likely to be reasonable and reachable.

~ * ~ * ~ * ~ * ~ * ~ * ~ * ~ * ~ * ~ * ~

A cookie-cutter approach to solving behavior problems cannot possibly work for every dog. The information and attention to detail provided in each chapter herein will allow you to customize a behavior modification plan that takes into account your dog's particular issues, and the unique aspects of your lifestyle. The interactive format is designed to encourage you to become a fully engaged participant in your dog's recovery. Rather than feeling overwhelmed by the problem, you will instead be enabled to gain the necessary confidence and skills to put your dog at ease.

First, you'll learn about what separation anxiety is—and what it isn't. The distinction is an important one because if, for example, your dog's symptoms are actually due to boredom or a lack of exercise, approaching the case as one of separation-related distress will not solve the problem. By considering carefully crafted questions and performing quick, easy experiments, you will determine whether your dog has a true separation issue and, if so, which type.

A brief discussion of possible causes follows. Then it's on to the Firm Foundation Program, which will help you to lay a solid base upon which a sound behavioral protocol can be built. The first pillar of the Program is management. You'll get plenty of creative "home alone" ideas for those times when you need to leave the house, whether briefly or for a longer period. Having a variety of options is crucial, because there is nothing so frustrating as feeling you are being held hostage in your own home!

The next two pillars of the Program are nutrition and exercise. Their role in keeping your dog calm and relaxed cannot be emphasized strongly enough. Even if you are well versed on the subjects, you might be surprised at some of the things you'll discover.

Developing confidence is the final pillar of the Program, and it's a pivotal one. You'll learn how to boost your dog's confidence in ways that will be fun for both of you. Increased self-confidence will allow your dog to cope more easily with difficult situations, including being left alone.

The potential benefits of medication in treating separation anxiety will also be discussed. While many dogs with separation issues can be rehabilitated without the use of drugs, for others, pharmacological intervention is the key that opens the door for behavior modification efforts to be successful.

Once a foundation has been laid, it's on to the Behavior Modification section, where a protocol will be tailored to your dog's individual needs. You will be able to determine where to start, at what pace you should work, and when to advance to the next level. Don't worry that the process will be complicated; it won't. Recording your progress along the way will help you to stay motivated and on track.

To solve complex behavior problems, it is sometimes necessary to think outside the box. To that end, the final section of this book explores tools and products with which you may not be familiar, but which might be just the thing to help your dog. The *Resources* section contains information on where to find each one, as well as extensive information on other helpful books, organizations, and products.

Throughout the book, you will find stories that were contributed by professional canine behavior specialists. Each narrative details how a particular dog's separation anxieties were addressed. Some cases concern a client's dog, while others involve the trainer's own dog. The issues range from mild or moderate to some that are more severe, including a dog whose anxiety drove her onto a third-story ledge! What all of the accounts have in common is that they will give you a better idea of how behavioral treatment plans look when implemented in real life, and what type of results can be achieved.

Solving your dog's separation issues will require patience and dedication, but rest assured, you can do it. After all, you're armed with a strong love for your dog and all the information you need. The reward for your efforts will be a dog who can remain home alone feeling calm and relaxed—and that will bring peace of mind to you both.

PART I
Overview

What Separation Anxiety is—and What it *Isn't*

Bob suspected that his ten-month-old Beagle, Rocky, had separation anxiety. He consulted his veterinarian, and Rocky was put on a course of drug therapy. The diagnosis had been reached on the basis of Rocky's destructive behavior when Bob was gone. Had Hurricane Rocky decimated everything in its path, leaving a trail of tattered evidence in its wake? No. In fact, the Beagle wasn't even consistently destructive. Most recently, after a week of being "good," Rocky had chewed a shoe. *One shoe*—and a lowly slipper at that! While the destruction of footwear is no cause for celebration, it's also no reason to jump to the conclusion that a dog has separation anxiety.

Katie, a woman who frequents our local dog park, recently sought my opinion as to whether her Doberman had separation anxiety. When I asked why she suspected the problem, she said that each day when she left the house, Ruby would lie on the couch with her head on her paws and give her a sad look. That was all! It did sound as though Ruby was a bit sad that Katie was leaving, but unless other worrisome behaviors accompanied the display, the mild sadness alone did not a case of separation anxiety make.

Bob and Katie are far from being the only folks to be confused as to what constitutes a separation issue. Just the other day, a potential training client called and began the conversation by saying that her eighteen-month-old Golden Retriever had separation anxiety. Cheryl explained that when she and her husband were away, Duke was left in the back yard with her two other dogs. When the couple returned home, Duke would jump like a wild man on the sliding glass door, frantic to greet them. Upon further questioning, Cheryl revealed that on two occasions she had been able to sneak back in without Duke knowing. Had he been barking? Pacing? Obsessively searching for her? Nope. He'd been fast asleep. This was a case of poor manners, not a separation issue.

There is no blood panel or other medical test that can determine whether a dog has a separation issue. Because the diagnosis is based on observation of physical and behavioral responses, it is important to understand what is considered normal in those areas. Your dog following you around the house, for example, does not necessarily indicate a separation problem. Sure, there are "Velcro dogs" who won't leave their owner's side and may become upset when left on the other side of a door, even momentarily. And it's true that clingy behavior may be part of a separation issue. But in and of itself, sticking close to family members is an example of a dog behaving according to his natural instincts, and is no more a conclusive sign of separation anxiety than is chewing a shoe.

What is Separation Anxiety?

The popular usage of the term "separation anxiety" denotes a condition where a dog becomes emotionally distraught when separated from a specific person or persons, or when he is left alone. In the first type, the agitation stems from a strong attachment to a particular individual or individuals from whom the dog cannot bear to be apart. In the second, the dog's distress is not attributable to an emotional bond, but is simply a reaction to being isolated. In many cases of the latter type, a dog will remain at ease if he is left with a person—most anyone will do. For some, even the presence of another dog is enough to instill calmness. Those dogs, rather than having true separation issues, are more accurately described as suffering from "isolation distress."

Many behaviorists lump issues of separation from specific individuals and isolation distress together, and instead make the distinction between mild-to-moderate "separation distress" and clinical level separation anxiety. The latter involves an extreme degree of emotional upheaval. These are often the cases where dogs bloody themselves trying to get out of crates, or crash through windows in attempts to follow their owners. For our purposes, we will use the general terms "separation issue," "separation problem," and the like to encompass all levels of anxiety, from mild to extreme. Those umbrella terms will include dogs with isolation distress as well as those who cannot handle being separated from specific people. We will, however, differentiate between intensity levels and types of distress as needed.

Separation Problem or Sock Party?

So how do you know whether your dog actually has a separation issue? After all, many dogs seem hyperattached to their owners, and when left alone, destroy things. But where one dog may be sad as his owners leave, another appears to be thinking, *Whoohoo! They're finally gone! Par-teee!* While the results of a Poochapalooza can look a lot like the aftermath of a bout of anxiety, one should not be mistaken for the other. Destruction, inappropriate elimination, and incessant vocalizing are some of the most common signs of a separation issue, but they must be assessed in context with the rest of the dog's behavior.

Many times the aforementioned activities are attributable to a lack of training, or are manifestations of boredom due to a shortage of mental and/or physical stimulation. If your dog is left alone with a reservoir of unspent energy and no "legal" ways to vent it, any resulting barking or destruction should not be viewed as certain proof of a separation issue.

In some cases, destructive efforts will be focused on exit points such as doors and windows, or on items belonging to owners. For example, you come home to find that your dog has chewed up a paperback book you were reading or a hand towel (items which retain your scent). Or your dog claws or chews at the door where you exited or the window that offers a view of your car pulling away. Those behaviors are more likely to be related to a separation issue than would an act such as chewing up a picture frame (unless it holds a photo of you and your dog cuddling, in which case you have an extremely clever and melancholy dog). Still, even scent-related or escape-focused actions are not conclusive evidence of a separation issue and must be assessed in context.

One identifying factor in the diagnosis of a true separation issue is that *stress-related behaviors occur each and every time the dog is left alone.* You might not, however, see evidence of the same behavior each time. For example, one day you might return home to find urine on your hardwood floors, and another, that a magazine you'd left lying on your coffee table is now lying in shreds. Consider the following common owner-absent behaviors. Each may be a facet of a separation problem, but can also occur for other reasons:

Inappropriate urination and/or defecation: Neither of these displays is uncommon when a dog is not housetrained. Some dogs relieve themselves indoors only when their owners are absent, because they know if they are caught in the act, they will be reprimanded. But soiling can also happen because a dog is upset about being left alone. If your dog is completely housetrained—when you're at home, you never walk into a room to find an accident—and yet your dog soils when home alone, the behavior *may* be due to a separation issue. (Medical issues should be ruled out as well.) Although some dogs dispose of the "evidence" before owners return, using a camcorder as recommended later in this chapter will allow you to know whether elimination has occurred.

Whining, barking, or howling: Young puppies, when separated from their parents, will whine, bark, or even howl. These vocalizations are meant to encourage the adults to return. Dogs who are anxious about being home alone will often utter a bark or series of barks, pause, and then repeat the pattern. If a dog keeps vocalizing until family members reappear, the behavior has been rewarded, so it is more likely to reoccur. Barking can also be due to boredom, or to being stimulated by sights or sounds in the environment. Loud barking or howling from a home alone dog can be especially troublesome, as it can lead to complaints from neighbors, and even action from local animal control agencies.

Destruction: Some dogs, when left solo, will chew socks, shoes, and just about anything they can get their paws on. The damage may be as insignificant as the previously mentioned slipper or, like one of my training clients, as major as a $3000 hearing aid! Many dogs with separation issues chew item that carry their owner's scent, which lingers on items that have been worn or handled. Many dogs make beds out of their owners' dirty laundry for this reason.

Outdoor destruction may take the form of chewing, or redecorating in the ever-popular moon crater motif, since digging can be a fun way for dogs to release pent-up energy. These things are not normally indicative of a separation issue; digging or chewing at the fence line, however, may be.

It's no fun to arrive home to find unpleasant surprises such as potty accidents or destroyed valuables, but if it happens, don't punish your dog! Whether he was acting out of anxiety or simply misbehaving, punishing him after the fact accomplishes nothing. Dogs learn by associating things that happen more or less concurrently; that's why we reward a dog for sitting by offering a treat immediately, rather than ten minutes later. Punishing your dog after the fact teaches him nothing—except, possibly, to fear your return.

Behavioral Displays

Following is a list of behaviors that may be seen if your dog has a separation issue. Some are characteristic of milder distress, while others are more often seen at the extreme end of the spectrum.

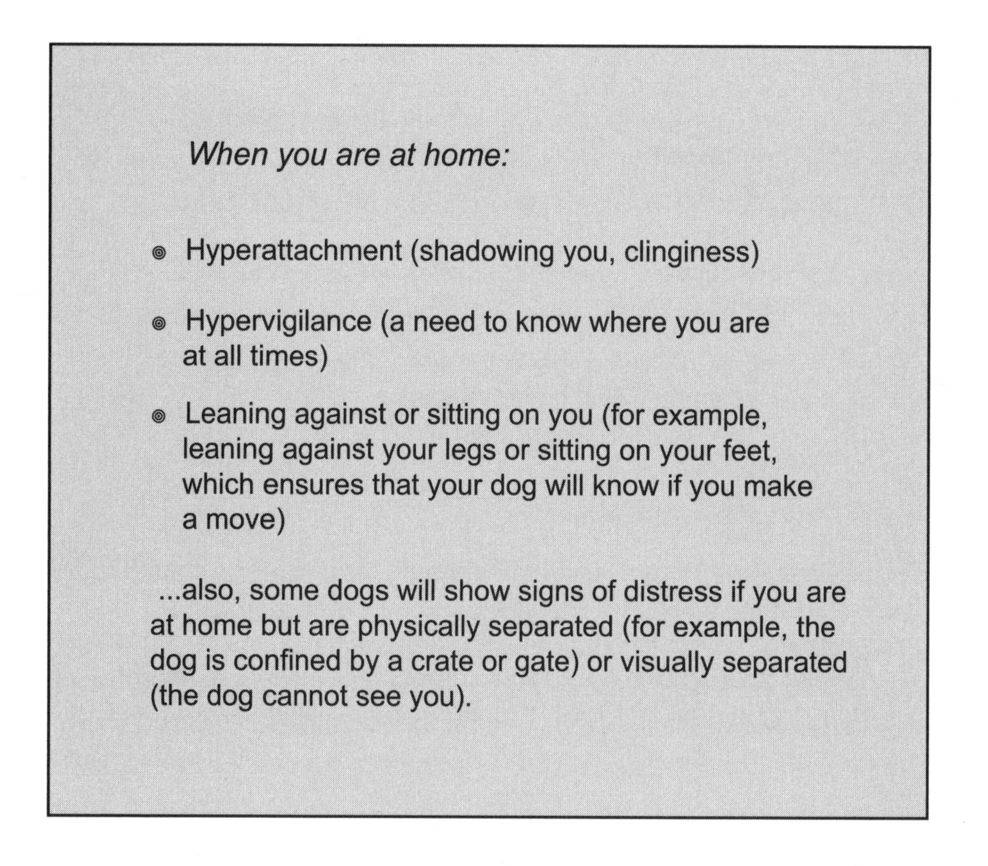

When you are at home:

- Hyperattachment (shadowing you, clinginess)
- Hypervigilance (a need to know where you are at all times)
- Leaning against or sitting on you (for example, leaning against your legs or sitting on your feet, which ensures that your dog will know if you make a move)

...also, some dogs will show signs of distress if you are at home but are physically separated (for example, the dog is confined by a crate or gate) or visually separated (the dog cannot see you).

When you are away:

- Inappropriate urination and/or defecation
- Destruction
- Vocalization – whining, barking, yelping, howling
- Pacing
- Clawing or chewing at exit points (doors, windows), or more extreme escape attempts (crashing through screens or windows)
- Shaking
- Drooling
- Diarrhea
- Panting
- Lack of appetite (a dog who is truly distressed will not eat, no matter how tasty the food)
- Vomiting
- Self-destructive behavior (chewing or licking at paws or other body parts)
- Digging at the fence line or chewing at wooden boards (in an attempt to find or follow you)
- Hyperactivity
- Depression, listlessness
- Obsessive compulsive behaviors (for example, spinning or flank-sucking)

…and, upon your return, manic greeting behavior, as though your dog is saying, *Gosh, I thought you'd never come back!*

Discovering Your Dog's Home Alone Activities

It is crucial that you are aware of exactly what you are dealing with as far as your dog's activities and emotional state when he is left alone. If your dog barks, for example, you'll want to know the intensity and duration of the behavior. If he is destructive, it will benefit you to be aware of whether the damage occurs in the first thirty minutes post-departure, or after a certain length of time.

I cannot stress strongly enough the importance of obtaining an accurate assessment of your dog's behavior during your absences. As previously mentioned, not long after we adopted Sierra, I'd noticed upon returning from errands that she was panting heavily—and we were not having hot weather. Setting up a camcorder was what allowed me to discover just how serious the issue was. We live in a rural area where our neighbors' homes are at a bit of a distance, and we all tolerate each other's dogs and other animals making noise now and then (not to mention the neighbor's son's heavy metal band!); no one complains. Because of this "live and let live" mentality, without the recording, I never would have known that Sierra had paced, barked and howled the entire time I was gone.

Set up a camcorder where it's likely to catch the most activity. (If you are unable to get your hands on a camcorder, use an audio recorder or a webcam. As a last resort, try to quietly sneak back to a window or other vantage point where you can see inside the house.) Leave your dog wherever you normally would when you're gone, whether that means crated, behind a gate, or loose in the house. Give him a chew item to keep him busy. Follow your normal departure routine. If you usually say something to your dog or pet him before leaving, do so; your actions should be as typical as possible. Leave the house, and stay away for a period that's usual for you. Upon your return, view the recording.

After reviewing the activity, note in detail what your dog did. Rather than ascribing emotions to what you saw—for example, "he seemed really sad," or, "I could tell he was upset," note only your dog's *actions*. Here is a sample response: "Jackson stood at the doorway for 30 seconds with his ear cocked after we left, then ran to the couch where I usually sit. He then jumped up and started burrowing into the cushions. After about two minutes, he picked up the television remote and chewed it.

For the next fifteen minutes he paced, and barked intermittently. He urinated. For the remaining ten minutes, his barking became louder and more excited. "

Below, write an account of what your dog did while you were gone:

____

____

____

____

____

____

____

Based on what you saw, would you say your dog has a true separation issue, or is it possible that he's simply bored? There is a difference between a dog who whines and paces incessantly, moving from door to window looking for you, and a dog who happily settles in to chew on a forbidden item, then takes a short nap. If it's not obvious what the behavior is attributable to (and don't feel badly if you can't tell for sure—it can be hard to discriminate), have a professional trainer review the recording. If you did observe what appears to be a true separation issue, would you classify it as mild, moderate, or extreme?

> No one wants to see their dog suffer, and watching the camcorder footage can be a difficult experience emotionally. Even if you don't engage the services of a professional dog trainer, have an objective friend or family member review the footage as well so you can get a better idea of whether your dog's stress level is mild, moderate, or truly extreme, without your subjective viewpoint influencing the assessment.

Differentiating Separation Anxiety from Isolation Distress

In order to construct an appropriate behavior modification and management plan, you must first determine whether your dog's distress is due to being separated from a particular person or persons, or is a reaction to being isolated. Unless you are already absolutely certain of the answer, perform the following experiments:

1. If there is more than one person living in the home, have the person your dog seems most attached to leave.

Is your dog still fairly calm as long as other people are present?

Sample responses:

◎ *I left but my husband stayed at home. Pogo watched my car pull away, then went to lie by my husband, who said Pogo seemed calm the whole time I was gone.*

◎ *Even though my husband was at home, Pogo still wouldn't settle down. He whined and periodically jumped up at the window where he'd seen me pull out of the driveway.*

____

____

____

____

____

____

2. Invite someone with whom your dog feels comfortable to your home. Arm the person with super yummy dog treats that take at least a few seconds each to chew. Retreat to another room and shut the door. Did

your dog take the treats? If he was extremely stressed about your leaving, he would not have eaten in your absence. This experiment does not rule out a separation issue, but helps to gauge the intensity level.

Sample responses:

◉ *My friend Nancy came over and Fizzy was willing to eat the treats as they sat together in the living room.*

◉ *Once I left the room, Fizzy began to whine and look for me. She totally ignored Nancy and the treats.*

____

____

____

____

____

____

3. This next experiment takes the previous one a step further. Invite someone who does not live with you but with whom your dog is comfortable to stay at your home while you and your housemates go out for a 15-20 minute walk. While you are gone, have the person offer your dog some super tasty treats. If your dog is toy-motivated, an attempt to engage your dog in play should be made as well.

Return home and ask for a report. What did your dog do?

Sample responses:

◉ *Our neighbor Ed came over to watch Kirby for 20 minutes. Ed said Kirby settled down very quickly after we left, and they played tug. When they were finished, Kirby happily took treats from Ed.*

◉ *Ed said Kirby was restless the entire time we were gone. He tried to get Kirby to play, but he wouldn't. Ed offered Kirby his favorite treats, but Kirby just paced and watched the front door.*

____

____

____

____

____

____

4. This next experiment applies if you only have one dog, as it is designed to test whether the presence of another dog will help to keep your dog calm. Set up your camcorder where it will pick up the most activity. Then have a friend drop their dog off for a while. (This should be a dog your dog knows and gets along with; do *not* leave your dog unsupervised with an unfamiliar dog.) When you return, review the results. Was your dog more relaxed in the presence of canine company?

Sample responses:

◉ *The dogs didn't even seem to notice we were gone! They spent most of the time playing and then resting together.*

◉ *Trixie ignored the other dog and lay by the door most of the time.*

____

____

____

____

Based on the results of your experiments, would you say your dog has a separation issue from a particular person or persons, or isolation distress? If the first experiment resulted in signs of stress when you were away, even if another family member was at home, your dog probably does have a specific-person(s)-centered separation issue. If, on the other hand, he was fine with another person for company, or another dog helped him to remain calm, your discoveries point toward isolation distress. Summarize your findings below.

____

____

____

____

____

____

____

____

____

____

____

The determinations you have made as to the type and intensity of your dog's separation issue will be used in creating potential management options and behavior modification plans. But before we begin to address the problem, let's take a look at how these issues start in the first place.

2

Possible Causes

When I was a child growing up in New York City, my mother often took me shopping to a popular department store called Alexander's. The outings were always a special treat, and thanks to the in-store restaurant, were probably also the origin of my unnaturally high regard for macaroni and cheese. My mother would flit happily from one sales rack to the next with me tagging along anticipating our lunch break. Unfortunately, Mom would sometimes get so engrossed in shopping that she forgot to check whether I was still beside her. Although I never ended up as the subject of an embarrassing loudspeaker announcement—"*We have a lost redheaded child at the manager's office*"—I did often end up separated from my mother for minutes at a time. I'll never forget how that initial anxiety at not being able to spot her turned to fear and then a rising panic as I frantically searched one aisle after another for her familiar silhouette. Perhaps it's partly due to those early experiences that I so empathize with the severe distress some dogs feel at being left all alone. Early traumatic experience is but one cause of canine separation issues.

Dogs have a natural inclination to bond with family members, so it's understandable that most crave companionship. Still, not all dogs develop separation issues. So what allows one dog to remain calm and cool when left solo, while another is reduced to a quivering mass of fur?

The Root of the Issue

Genetics: Every dog is born with a genetic blueprint that predisposes him to possess particular physical characteristics, as well as certain personality traits. Some dogs are naturally more inclined to be outgoing and friendly, and will boldly go forth into new situations with a healthy curiosity and perhaps even a sense of excitement. Those who inherit a less secure temperament may be shy or fearful in new environments or when greeting unfamiliar dogs or people. It stands to reason that dogs who are genetically predisposed to a general lack of confidence may have a difficult time coping with spending time alone.

> In her book *Clinical Behavioral Medicine for Small Animals*, veterinary behaviorist Karen Overall discusses the phenomenon of separation anxiety being commonly reported in studies of guide dogs. Guide dogs enjoy the company of humans from the time they are weaned, and because of that, popular conjecture held that the constant companionship itself caused separation issues. But as Dr. Overall states, "It is important to realize that these puppies were not unrelated to each other, but the puppy-raisers were. It is far more likely that the similarity that accounts for much of the consistency in the behavioral problems, which are all related to anxiety, is the one associated with the relatedness of the dogs, not the behaviors of the people." In other words, the separation issues were most likely due to a genetic predisposition to anxiety in the breeding lines, rather than anything the puppy-raisers did or did not do.

Dr. James Serpell, author and Director of the Center for the Interactions of Animals and Society at the University of Pennsylvania, acknowledges that "selectively breeding increasingly affectionate, socially dependent, and infantilized dogs may concomitantly select for excessive attachment to owners and intolerance to being alone."[1] Still, even if a dog is genetically predisposed to insecurity or anxiety, it does not mean the situation is hopeless. Just as dogs who are nervous around other dogs from a young age can become conditioned to remain calm in their presence, we can help to build the confidence of insecure dogs, and teach productive coping skills so they become better able to deal with isolation.

Assimilation: While constant companionship may not cause a separation issue, contrasting levels of attention during the period of assimilation into the family may do so. For example, the Dearborn family decides to get a puppy. They adopt Buster, a cute Cocker Spaniel, during summer break when teens Eddie and Cindy are on school vacation. Since family members' schedules overlap, someone is always at home during the day to see to Buster's physical needs and to monitor his behavior. This constant supervision proves helpful in many ways. But then vacation is over and the kids return to school. Buster is suddenly no longer enjoying roughhousing in the yard with Eddie, or cuddling on the couch with Cindy; he's left completely alone for hours at a time. The contrast between the continuous attention to which Buster has become accustomed and the total, abrupt isolation that follows is more than he can handle, and a separation issue is born. Dogs must learn *frustration tolerance*—that, as the Rolling Stones so eloquently put it, "You can't always get what you want." We will be teaching your dog to tolerate being alone, which is best accomplished in small doses.

Abandonment/Rehoming: A classic scenario for the development of separation problems is one in which a dog has been abandoned or rehomed. Many dogs are purchased or adopted as adorable young pups, only to be given up when they display not-so-adorable behavior problems at adolescence. Some are surrendered to shelters, given away, or even dumped on the streets when their owners decide they simply no longer have time to care for them. In some cases, dogs become victims of circumstance when their owners divorce or move to a new residence that does not allow dogs.

Regardless of the cause, the experience of being rehomed can be extremely difficult on an emotional level. Try to recall the warm feelings of security you experienced as a child, and how your home and family provided a base of strength from which you could operate in the world. Now imagine that in an instant, it's all gone. You suddenly find yourself in an unfamiliar living environment with people you don't know, no clue as to what's expected of you, and no idea of what's going to happen next. A dog who has lost his home is bereft not only of his loved ones, but also of the security of familiar surroundings and a known routine. Adrift, the dog may become clingy and needy toward human or canine family members.

A dog who has been rehomed will most likely become comfortable with his new family over time, but might still feel a lingering insecurity about being left alone, especially if he has gone from a home with another dog to one where he is completely isolated when his people are away. And for a dog who has been abandoned—for example, the family moved and left the dog in the yard or house—it can be even more stressful to be alone in a new home, even for short periods, as the dog must wonder whether his new family will return at all. In short, some dogs who have been rehomed or abandoned may fear that temporary separation equals desertion.

While it's true that some dogs who are adopted from shelters have separation issues, there are many who assimilate easily into new homes and don't mind being left on their own. Adopting from a shelter or rescue group is a noble and compassionate act, and millions of owners would attest that it's one of the best things they've ever done.

Breed: Although hard scientific evidence on the topic is scant, some have theorized that separation anxiety may be more prevalent in certain breeds. Herding and hunting dogs, for example, have been specifically bred to do jobs that require a strong bond of cooperation with, and therefore attachment to, people. Companion dogs were created to be just that, making a desire for constant closeness with people more likely than it would be in dogs who were bred to do a solitary job such as guarding livestock. Regardless, separation anxiety can affect dogs of any breed.

Traumatic Experience: If a frightening event—an earthquake or a burglary, for example—occurs when a dog is home by himself, it could cause the dog to develop a fear of being left alone in the house. One of my clients' dogs was home alone when a fire broke out. He came out of it physically unharmed, but the psychological trauma left him with a challenging case of separation anxiety.

Sometimes the anxiety-producing disturbance is less dramatic, such as a faulty security alarm going off, a thunderstorm, or even a startling noise from a nearby construction site. Still, it leaves enough of a lasting impression on the dog that he becomes nervous about being left in the house. If there is no obvious cause of your dog's separation distress and the onset is sudden, it is worthwhile to consider whether some change in the environment could be a contributing factor.

Any sudden separation—for example, becoming lost as a puppy—can be traumatizing. Even being left at a boarding kennel is enough of a jarring experience for some dogs to develop separation issues. If an owner who is home much of the time suddenly has to be gone for days or weeks, the dog finds himself for all intents and purposes abandoned, as he does not realize the separation is temporary.

Another type of traumatic experience can occur when a puppy is removed too early from the birth mother. According to Dr. James Serpell, this type of premature separation may cause future difficulties with routine separations.[1] While some dispute this theory, unless you acquired your dog as a very young puppy, you won't know whether early separation might have played a part.

Aging: Senior dogs, just like elderly people, are prone to developing various ailments and infirmities. Sometimes these challenges are at the root of a separation issue. If a dog experiences sight and/or hearing loss, for example, he may become clingy in an attempt to reassure himself about his surroundings.

Cognitive dysfunction is another common malady of senior dogs. A three-year study by Chapman & Voith[2] focused on behavior problems in 26 dogs aged ten or older. Ten of the dogs displayed destructive behavior, ten exhibited inappropriate urination, defecation, or both, and seven vocalized excessively. While those behaviors can certainly be attributable to cognitive dysfunction alone, of the 26 dogs studied, 13 were diagnosed with separation anxiety. If your dog has never showed any signs of separation distress, but is now a senior and is displaying unusual behaviors, discuss the possibility of cognitive dysfunction with your veterinarian. In some cases nutritional intervention, supplements, anti-anxiety medications, or other drugs can be helpful.

Dr. Nicholas Dodman, author and Director of the Animal Behavior Clinic at Tufts Cummings School of Veterinary Medicine, differentiates between canine cognitive dysfunction and what he terms "nocturnal separation anxiety."[3] With the latter condition, there are no signs of cognitive decline, but dogs appear hypervigilant and anxious at night. Dr. Dodman states that in all the cases he has encountered, once cognitive dysfunction and noise phobias were ruled out, the cause was found to be a painful medical condition that had not been obvious. Some of those included tumors of the brain, bone, bladder, or eye, and severe spinal arthritis. As Dr. Dodman mentions, people battling cancer often suffer from nocturnal anxiety, and dogs probably do for the same reason: at night, there is nothing to distract them from their suffering. If you suspect nocturnal separation anxiety, a veterinary exam is in order.

A Common Misconception

With all this talk about the possible causes of separation issues, what is *not* responsible for these problems bears mentioning as well. There is a common misconception that allowing a dog to sleep in one's bed, or showing too much attention or affection to a dog, will create a separation issue. This is untrue. According to Dr. Karen Overall, "Studies that have examined client behavior and the development of separation anxiety have demonstrated no association between the former and the development of the latter (Voith & Borchelt, 1985; Voith et. al., 1992)." She also states that, "Studies specifically seeking to find causal associations between client attachment to their pet and separation anxiety have failed to do so (Jagoe & Serpell, 1996; Serpell, 1987)."

More recently, Valli Parsatharasy and Sharon Crowell-Davis studied 32 dogs with and 43 dogs without owner-reported separation anxiety. After a formal attachment test, the dogs were videotaped for 30 minutes while alone at home. The researchers came to the conclusion that "separation anxiety is not based on 'hyperattachment' of the dog to the owner."[4] That said, some dog owners behave in such a way that the formation of an overly attached relationship is encouraged. Although such an intense bond may not *cause* a problem, it does not mean that it can't exacerbate an existing separation issue.

~ * ~ * ~ * ~ * ~ * ~ * ~ * ~ * ~ * ~ * ~

Regardless of whether your dog's separation issue is due to genetics, early environmental factors, a traumatic incident, or life experience, rest assured, in most cases, vast improvements can be made.

1 Serpell, J, Fagoe JA: Early experience and the development of behaviour, in Serpell J (ed): *The Domestic Dog: Its Evolution, Behaviour, and Interactions with People.* Cambridge, Cambridge University Press, 1995, pp 80-102

2 Chapman BL, Voith VL: Behavioral problems in old dogs: 26 cases (1984-1987). *JAVMA* 196:944-946, 1990.

3 Dr. Nicholas Dodman, Medical Causes and Treatment of Behavior, Temperament, and Training Problems, *The APDT Chronicle of the Dog*, March/April 2010, p.21

4 Parthasarathy, V., Crowell-Davis, S.: Relationship between attachment to owners and separation anxiety in pet dogs (*Canis lupus familiaris*) (2006) *Journal of Veterinary Behavior* 1:3 (109-120)

PART II

The Firm Foundation Program

The Firm Foundation Program

The goal of the Firm Foundation Program is to create a solid base on which a successful behavior modification protocol can be built. The four pillars of the program are management, nutrition, exercise, and confidence building. The importance of establishing good practices in each of these areas should not be underestimated, as they will contribute to your dog's overall sense of calm and confidence as well as his general health and well being. A calm, confident, healthy dog will have an enhanced ability to handle stress.

This section ends with a chapter on pharmacological intervention. It is not one of the four pillars, but you will soon see why it is included. To be clear, I am not suggesting that your dog needs drug therapy; still, it bears mentioning, as in some cases it is helpful or even necessary.

As you read through each chapter, consider your dog's current lifestyle and assess how well it matches the recommendations that are offered. If you find there are multiple changes you'd like to make, don't feel pressured to switch everything at once. You might discover that all you need to do for now is gradually switch your dog's diet and implement a new style of management when you're away. Or, you might begin to increase your dog's exercise, and take him to training classes that will bolster his confidence. As you'll see, the program is designed in a way that allows you to tailor it to your dog's individual needs as well as to your own lifestyle. The suggestions are easy to implement—after all, the idea is to decrease stress, not add to it!

By virtue of the framework you lay now, your behavior modification efforts will be that much more successful.

3

Management in the Meantime

An important part of the behavior modification plan for treating separation issues involves planned departures. By leaving the house for very short periods, and then lengthening those periods in small increments, you will help your dog learn to feel comfortable when left alone. The approach could be summed up as, "A little at a time so your dog feels fine." Because the process is gradual, with each bit of success building on the previous one, it would not do for you to suddenly leave your dog home alone for a longer period than he could handle. For that reason, it is vitally important that you find suitable management options.

Environmental management can be one of the more challenging parts of any separation rehabilitation program. Not leaving your dog alone other than during preplanned departures may mean that you'll have to miss going to the movies with your spouse for a while; that you'll skip lunch dates with friends; and that spontaneous weekend trips will be temporarily on hold.

Know in advance that you may feel trapped. You may even feel resentment toward your dog, and wonder whether all you are doing is worthwhile. If the situation becomes frustrating, just remember that these are short-term sacrifices that will allow your dog to become more emotionally stable over time, and to have a better quality of life. Think of it as one more thing you do because you love your dog. Besides, the efforts you make now will also decrease *your* stress levels in the long run.

Management Options

Which management solutions are viable depends on your lifestyle, and on whether your dog has isolation distress, or anxiety over being separated from you or other individuals.

Keeping in mind that these are temporary measures, here are some suggestions:

1. When you need to run errands, bring your dog along. Many dogs feel less stressed when left in the car than at home, because they learn that you always return quickly to the car. Park where your dog can see you enter the store, house, or wherever you're going. (Never leave your dog in the car on a hot day. It takes mere seconds for the interior temperature to reach life-threatening levels, even with the windows slightly rolled down.) If your dog is nervous when left in the car even for short periods, try a pressure wrap (see *Chapter17*).

2. You can still get together with friends, but do it at canine-friendly places so you can bring your dog along. Meet at a local park; stroll around an outdoor shopping plaza; or, have a chat over coffee at an outdoor cafe. (Part of the amazing success of Starbucks must surely be due to the number of coffee drinkers who enjoy hanging out there with their dogs. Give it a try—you might just become as addicted to relaxing outdoors with your furry friend as you are to your morning java.) There are even restaurants with outdoor patios that allow dogs to accompany their owners, so don't deny yourself a nice lunch or dinner out.

> The website www.dogfriendly.com covers most major cities, and lists pet-friendly restaurants and cafes, hotels, beaches, parks, stores, and attractions. You could even take your dog with you on vacation. If you don't have internet access or prefer a hard copy, consider purchasing the book *Dogfriendly.com's U.S. and Canada Travel Guide* (see *Resources*).

3. If your dog has isolation distress and having another dog present helped to keep him calm, assuming your dog gets along with unfamiliar dogs, allow him to spend a fun-filled day (or part of a day, at first) at a doggy daycare center. An added benefit of allowing your dog to play with others is that he'll come home tired, which will automatically lessen his stress levels—and yours.

4. Arrange for play dates. You could alternate between a friend's home and yours, and make it a regular event. Whether or not the humans need to be present depends upon whether your dog is anxious when left with another dog, the level of destruction the dogs are prone to, and the home environment. If, for example, your neighbor has a safe, enclosed yard without a pool, and the weather is cool enough, the dogs might be fine left outside. But if your dog needs human companionship, someone should be at home the entire time.

5. Let's say you don't have any friends who have dog-friendly dogs. Not to worry; there are plenty of dogs out there who don't want to be left alone. Post a notice online or in your community seeking a dog to keep yours company during the days, or whenever you are normally gone. You might just end up with a lot more replies than you expected. Meet with people and their dogs a few times first at a local park or other public place to ensure that the dogs get along well, and that you feel the person is trustworthy.

Before you decide to leave your dog at a home other than your own, check the area where he will spend time. What serves as adequate backyard fencing for one dog may not be sufficient to contain another. Walk the perimeter. Check down low for holes or openings, and up high for places your dog could scale or jump over. Garbage cans and other objects should be far enough from walls that they can't serve as launch pads. All gates should have padlocks; you don't want to return to find that your dog was let out by a child or through the negligence of a gardener or other service person. If there is a pool, there should be fencing around it so the dogs cannot fall in. Ensure too that the area where your dog will be kept has shade, shelter, and plenty of water. If your dog will be allowed indoors, do a quick check for potentially toxic or hazardous items he could get into. Just because the resident dog leaves them alone, that doesn't mean yours won't try to investigate.

6. Assuming a case of isolation distress, arrange for a friend or relative to come over and spend a few hours with your dog. That might sound odd, but it's important for your own mental health during this process to get out of the house now and then to do something fun. If you don't know anyone who could help, hire a professional pet sitter. There are organizations (see *Resources*) that can help you to find one in your area. If you can't locate a pet sitter, hire a human babysitter who is dog-friendly; your dog will be happy, and the sitter will be relieved that she doesn't have to change diapers!

7. Here's a creative emergency measure: drop your dog off at the groomer. Most groomers will spend at least two to three hours brushing, bathing, clipping, ear hair plucking, and doing whatever else is needed. Now, dogs don't need to be groomed more often than every four to six weeks (get an individual recommendation based on your dog's coat), and the groomer is not a dog sitter. But if your dog hasn't been groomed for a while and you're out of options, a little primping can save the day.

8. Another emergency measure to consider is day boarding at a kennel or veterinary hospital. Of course, this alternative is only feasible if your dog is tolerant of being crated or caged.

9. This next suggestion falls under the category of Sneaky Leaving. The goal is to be able to leave the house for a short period without your dog even knowing you're gone. The technique is possible only if you have a dog who is already at the point where he can be separated from you by sight and proximity; for example, he's calm being in the yard alone while you're in the house, or feels comfortable being crated in another room while you go about your business. It is also probably easier to execute if you live in a house than in an apartment-type setting.

a. Using a digital recorder, make a "Sounds of Home" audio recording that includes the types of noises your dog is apt to hear when you're present. It might include water running as you do dishes, footsteps, you chatting on the phone, the television, or whatever else would be heard on a typical day. Try to make it all sound as unrehearsed and realistic as possible, and be sure there are short periods of silence as would naturally occur. Record for 30-60 minutes, or however long you can. As you prepare to leave, set your "Sounds of Home" creation to play on endless loop.

b. Now comes the sneaky part, which involves turning the recording on, and exiting the house without your dog realizing you've left. Be sure your dog is in an area where he can hear the recording but will not have access to the space it's in. For example, your dog is locked out in the yard but the sounds will be coming from inside the house, which is where you place the recorder before you leave. In an apartment, you'll have to confine your dog, preferably with music playing to screen out the sound of you leaving. The recorder will then be placed in an out of sight area.

Open the front door and shut it behind you as quietly as possible. (If you've got squeaky door hinges, oil them first.) If you're in an apartment, you may now be home free, as you can just walk down the hall or take the elevator and your dog will be none the wiser. If you're in a house, however, and you need to make a vehicular getaway, either:

i. Leave the car parked a short distance away the night before so you can walk to it and start the engine without your dog realizing it's you; or, if you're lucky enough to have two vehicles, keep one parked a short distance away, and walk to it.

ii. If you live on a hill or slope, put the car in neutral and coast for a short distance before turning on the ignition. Sneaky but effective!

Your Plan

Through careful consideration, you should be able to come up with a plan that fits your lifestyle. Below is a sample plan for Linda, who works outside the home five days a week. Her Boxer mix Tyson is social with dogs and people.

Mon./Wed./Fri.:	Tyson will go to Daycamp for Dogs.
Tuesdays:	He'll go to neighbor Denise's house to play with her dog Duke.
Thursdays:	Choice of Bill's apartment or calling pet sitter Beth to come and stay with him.
Weekends/days off:	I'll take Tyson with me for short errands. For longer absences, I'll have someone stay with him at the apartment, or drop him at Denise's or Bill's. Or, in a pinch, he can go get groomed!

Note some management options that seem feasible, along with specific resources such as friends and neighbors:

What About Adding a Second Dog?

If your dog has isolation distress, you might be wondering whether getting a second dog could provide the ultimate management solution. The answer is *maybe*. If you truly do not want a second dog and would only be getting one to keep your first dog company, don't do it, as it might not fix the problem. If, on the other hand, you'd like to add another four-footed member to your family anyway, go for it! If your first dog is young and playful, at the very least, having another dog to play with will help to burn off some of that energy. A well-exercised dog is a calmer dog. Just be sure the new dog is confident and comfortable when being left alone, lest you end up with twice the problem.

Lila's Story

Victoria Stilwell, dog trainer and star of Animal Planet's "It's Me or the Dog," relates how getting a second dog solved a separation issue for one of her clients:

My client, Maya Adams, lived in an apartment in Manhattan. Lila, her four-year-old female greyhound, suffered anxiety each time Maya went out. Lila would whine, bark, chew, and lick the back of the front door until Maya returned. Neighbors reported that the barking would last for hours.

It was clear to me that Lila was suffering from separation anxiety, and for many months Maya and I worked to alleviate the stress Lila felt when left alone. Even though her behavior improved, she still found it hard to settle by herself, leaving us to consider whether getting another dog to keep her company would help the situation. I was reticent to recommend this, as dogs that suffer distress when separated can have such an attachment to their owners; the presence of another dog does nothing to calm them.

Fortunately, in this case a companion dog turned out to be the answer. Eddie, a five-year-old male greyhound, joined the family and almost immediately Lila relaxed. The change was profound and proved to me that for some dogs who suffer from separation anxiety, a companion animal can help where behavioral therapy can't.

Getting a second dog is more likely to solve the problem if the first dog has isolation distress (as opposed to separation issues from a particular person), as in the story that follows.

Morgan's Story Helen Hollander, CPDT-KA

Mogul, my husband's and my beloved Great Dane, had died. Morgan, our three-year-old Airedale, pined for days over the absence of his soul mate. However, because I was home with an infant, he never lacked companionship and soon became my shadow. He loved the baby, felt safe with me, and life was grand… until one day, when Morgan and I went to visit my mother.

As soon as I entered her home, a man jumped out from around a corner of the entry hall and put a knife to my throat. Morgan began to growl. That's when the man took the knife away from my throat...and dug it into Morgan's throat! He told me to shut the dog up "or else." I immediately told the robber I'd give him whatever he wanted, and pleaded with him not to hurt my dog. I told Morgan to hush and he did, although I knew he could sense my tremendous fear and anxiety. The robber instructed me to give him money. I did, and he fled, leaving both of our lives traumatically changed in the wake.

Morgan had always been fine if left with a "sitter," but whenever he was all by himself, he showed destructive tendencies. Although my own fear and anxiety had diminished over time after the incident, Morgan was out of control. The destructive behavior escalated. He began chewing pillows; he dug holes in the carpet; he ate through the baseboards of the wall, and through the wall to the studs! And he managed to chew through a metal crate, inflicting severe wounds on his body. (We no longer used a crate after that.)

Ultimately, we returned home from an early dinner to find Morgan sitting outside on our doorstep. How could that be? While we were out, Morgan had managed the great escape. He literally dove through a glass window and screen, most probably in search of us. I realized then that this dog was suffering from severe separation anxiety. Whether it was triggered by the loss of his soul mate, the robbery incident, or a combination of both, he was suffering. After 32 years, I still have pangs of guilt...if only I knew then what I know now.

Regardless, I realized Morgan needed help. But what kind of help? Growing up in the company of dogs my entire life did not prepare me for this “special needs” dog. I read books and articles and tried all the usual protocols to help Morgan “be alone.” Nothing worked and my heart broke for him.

One day (don’t ask me what I was thinking), I brought home a Wheaten Terrier puppy. Morgan was smitten with Bogie. Being the gentle dog that he was, he would follow the puppy around endlessly and sleep beside his crate as if he was the appointed puppy nanny. The two dogs became inseparable and my life slowly became less stressful. Was this what he needed? As a professional trainer these days, this would not be my first suggestion. However, for Morgan’s insecurity, I have to answer yes. Morgan needed a stable mate.

Morgan died at the age of 14. We quickly filled his shoes with a neurotic but loving German Shepard Dog named “Shadow.” Need I say more? I never have less than two dogs these days.

Morgan and Mogul

Nutrition

You're probably wondering what on earth your dog's diet has to do with his stress levels when left alone. The answer is, plenty. Have you ever drank one cup of coffee too many and gotten that jittery, wired feeling? You might have snapped at your co-workers, been more impatient than usual when waiting in line, or reacted with vitriol when someone cut you off in traffic. Likewise, have you noticed the way kids act when they've eaten too much sugar? They can become cranky and hyperactive. What we ingest has a direct effect on our nervous system. A long-term diet of sweets and processed foods will surely impact our health, but it may also cause us to feel less emotionally balanced, and even depressed, anxious, or angry. By the same token, eating a healthful diet contributes to a state of well being both physically and emotionally. It's no different for dogs.

Dog food that is built on inferior protein sources and laden with unhealthy chemicals, preservatives, and excess sugars can contribute to issues such as hyperactivity, restlessness, and nervousness. Remember, the idea of the Firm Foundation program is for your dog to feel as relaxed as possible across the board. A healthful diet will go a long way toward allowing your dog to feel physically calmer, which will set the stage for a tranquil emotional state. Making wise nutritional choices will also result in better overall health for your dog, which will be especially beneficial as he ages.

> If your dog has a medical condition, discuss any potential dietary changes with your veterinarian.

Most people opt to feed their dogs pre-packaged, dry kibble. Some feed canned food, and others, a combination of wet and dry. A smaller percentage of owners choose a raw diet, or cook for their dogs. My book *Help for Your Fearful Dog* (see *Resources*) includes a discussion of nutrition that covers each of those options. I have reprinted a portion of the text below, with a few updates.

Become Label Able

There are so many dog foods on the market and so many claims made by manufacturers that it can be difficult to figure out which products are truly nutritious. One brand is said to have "scientifically balanced ingredients," while another claims to "turn back the hands of time" and restore your dog to a younger, healthier state. (Let's face it, if there were truth in advertising, no woman would have a single wrinkle!) Learning to read labels will allow you to bypass exaggerated advertising claims and to accurately assess quality.

By law, dog food manufacturers must list ingredients in descending order by bulk weight. For example, a bag of dry kibble that lists the first three ingredients as "chicken meal, chicken by-product meal, rice" has more chicken meal than any other ingredient. Because dogs are primarily carnivores, the first two ingredients should consist of meat.

> Beware! Some sneaky manufacturers break less-than-ideal ingredients into parts so they appear lower on the list. For example, a label might read, "chicken meal, ground corn, corn meal, corn gluten meal." In reality, if all of the corn products were grouped together and listed as one ingredient, "corn" would have to be listed first because of its bulk weight.

The most common meat sources used in dog foods in the United States are chicken, turkey, lamb, and beef. (Some brands now offer organic meat sources, which are more expensive but worth the cost.) There are three basic grades of meat. Using chicken as an example, the highest grade would simply be labeled "chicken." This indicates a whole meat source—the clean flesh of slaughtered chickens, limited to lean muscle tissue. A step below that is "chicken meal," which is made from rendered muscle and tissue. (Rendering is the process that separates fat-soluble from water-soluble materials, removes most of the water, and may destroy or alter some of the natural enzymes and proteins found in raw ingredients.) If "meal" is listed, the source should be identified, rather than the vaguely descriptive "poultry meal" or "meat meal."

The lowest grade of meat is "by-products." Chicken by-products may include heads, feet, undeveloped eggs, and intestines. Foods that contain by-products, especially when they appear early on the list of ingredients, are not high quality. (For more on what goes into dog foods, read *Food Pets Die For* by Ann Martin—see *Resources*.)

Avoid dog foods that contain large amounts of corn. Many manufacturers use corn as a main source of protein, since it is less expensive than meat. It is also, however, a common allergen that has been known to cause dry, itchy skin.

Corn can also, through a series of chemical reactions in the body, affect serotonin levels. Serotonin is a neurotransmitter that is manufactured in the brains of both dogs and people. It has many functions, including the regulation of mood. Have you ever noticed how calm and even lethargic people become after a Thanksgiving dinner? That's because turkey contains tryptophan, an amino acid that is a precursor to serotonin. Many researchers believe there is a direct link between serotonin imbalance and depression in humans. That's why depression is often treated with a class of drugs known as Selective Serotonin Reuptake Inhibitors (SSRIs), which affect levels of serotonin in the brain.

James O'Heare, Ph.D., author and president of the Companion Animal Sciences Institute, calls serotonin "the happy messenger" and believes that increasing its levels in a dog's brain may significantly reduce stress, anxiety, and aggression. Corn, on the other hand, is high in the amino acid tyrosine. O'Heare refers to tyrosine as the "anti-tryptophan." In short, because corn makes it harder for the amino acids necessary for the production of serotonin to pass through the blood-brain barrier, it is not conducive to a calm state of mind.

Other ingredients to avoid include artificial colors or flavors, and any that are not identified by source (for example, "animal fat" rather than "chicken fat"). Also, read the ingredient line that begins "preserved with…" The desirable preservatives are vitamins E (sometimes listed as "mixed tocopherols") and C (often called "ascorbic acid"). The unhealthful, potentially cancer-causing preservatives are BHA, BHT, and ethoxyquin, which are, unfortunately, still used in some pet foods.

In general, supermarket brands are of lower quality than those found at pet supply stores. Higher quality foods cost more initially, but because they contain more nutrients, less is fed per meal. (And because the body is able to absorb more of the nutrients, less waste product is produced—a bonus for the poop-scoopers among us.) Feeding a high quality food is an investment in your dog's health. Spending a bit more now might well save you the cost of veterinary visits in the future.

The Dog Food Project website (see *Resources*) features excellent articles on canine nutrition, thorough information on which ingredients to avoid, and an up-to-date listing of foods that have been recalled. It also offers detailed ingredient lists, protein content and more for most brands of dry kibble sold in retail stores, making it easy to assess and compare the food you're currently feeding.

If you decide to switch foods, do it gradually over the course of a week. Increase the amount of the new product gradually as you decrease the quantity of the old one. For example, feed a mixture of 1/4 new to 3/4 old for a few days; 1/2 and 1/2 for the next few days; then 3/4 new to 1/4 old; and finally, all new. Although changing foods now and then is beneficial as far as varying protein sources, switching too rapidly or constantly changing foods carries the risk of causing gastrointestinal problems.

Can It

There has long been a perception that canned dog foods are less nutritious than dry kibble, but more and more manufacturers are now producing superior canned products. As long as a high quality food is chosen, and the dog has other chewing outlets to keep his jaws and teeth healthy, canned-only can be a perfectly healthful option. In fact, canned foods tend to be fresher than dry kibble, generally have higher quality ingredients, and contain fewer chemicals and preservatives. And canned foods almost always contain a higher percentage of meat than dry kibble does.

Just as with dry food, quality varies greatly from brand to brand, so a bit of sleuthing is necessary. Look for a whole meat source to be listed as the first ingredient. Some mid-to-lower quality foods list water as the first ingredient. Most premium canned foods use meat, poultry, or fish broth in place of water. The same rules that apply when evaluating the ingredients in kibble are applicable when investigating canned foods.

The Whole Dog Journal periodically reviews dog food brands and names its top picks. Visit www.whole-dog-journal.com for a list of past articles that are available for download. Even better, subscribe so you can stay up to date on new information.

In the Raw

Some owners forego processed foods altogether and instead feed a raw diet. The staple of the typical plan is raw, meaty bones—chicken or turkey backs and necks, cow femur "marrow bones," and other forms of raw meat. The diet also includes pulverized raw vegetables and other healthful foods. Proponents of raw feeding credit the diet with being responsible for overall enhanced canine health and increased longevity, improved behavior, and even recovery from disease. Some veterinarians caution against raw diets, citing the possibility of a bone perforating a dog's intestine or stomach, or causing broken teeth or choking. Those problems can be avoided by grinding the meat, bones and all. Many butchers will do the grinding for you.

The most popular canine raw diet goes by the unfortunate acronym BARF—Biologically Appropriate Raw Food, or Bones And Raw Food. If you plan to try raw feeding, research carefully to ensure that the diet is properly balanced and that you add the right supplements in the correct amounts. Purchase meat that is free of hormones and antibiotics; if you can find and afford organic meats, even better. Use safe handling procedures, and check with your veterinarian to make sure your nutritional plan will be safe for your dog. (For books on raw feeding, see *Resources*.)

Commercial Frozen Diets

There are a number of companies that offer ready-to-eat (or almost-ready-to-eat), meat-based frozen foods. These commercially prepared products are convenient and make it easy to ensure that your dog is getting a proper nutritional balance. Some manufacturers offer complete meals that have been freeze-dried and require nothing more than adding water. Others produce mixtures of vegetables and other nutrients that can be added to a meat-based diet. Some products can be found at local pet supply stores, while others must be mail ordered. (See *The Whole Dog Journal* website for recent articles and reviews of individual brands.)

That Down Home Cookin'

When we first brought Sierra home, she suffered from gastrointestinal issues. I began to cook for her, and somehow I never stopped. Preparing her meals comprises the sum total of my culinary skills. What I'm doing is probably technically not so much cooking as it is browning meat in a skillet, adding hot water to a pre-made veggie mix, and stirring in a bit of oil and a vitamin mix. What I'm saying is, if I can do it, you can too.

Boiled chicken, vegetables, and other healthful foods are infinitely more nutritious for your dog than what is found in most dry dog foods. If you choose to feed a homemade diet, pay careful attention to nutritional balance and consider whether supplements are necessary. There are helpful books available that contain recipes, information on supplementation, and considerations for dogs with specific medical needs. (See *Resources*.) If your dog has a medical condition, again, a veterinary consult is in order before you implement any dietary changes.

~ * ~ * ~ * ~ * ~ * ~ * ~ * ~ * ~ * ~ * ~

As you can see, ensuring that your dog eats a healthy, balanced diet can take a bit of time and research, but it's well worth it. Even without doing any behavior modification exercises, within a few weeks of switching to a more healthful diet, you may notice that your dog seems more relaxed and at ease, which will translate to his being that much calmer when you're away.

Exercise

Imagine that you're scheduled to take a written exam. You've studied hard; still, you're nervous. The morning of the test arrives. You wake, spend thirty minutes on the treadmill, and lift some light weights. You eat a healthful breakfast and then hit the road. Your pleasantly tired out body and settled stomach contribute to an overall feeling of calm during the test. You ace it!

But wait—let's envision this scene again with a different beginning. You stay up late the night before the exam, skip breakfast, and decide you don't have time to exercise. Instead, you down two quick cups of coffee, and gulp another on the way. Throughout the test, you restlessly tap your foot, adjust your seating position, and nervously edge your way through question after question. Your test score? Not as good as it could have been. In the first scenario, while the morning exercise and meal didn't directly cause you to recall more information, it allowed your body to be at ease, which took the edge off your nervous emotional state. The physical relaxation allowed you to perform better, and it made a potentially nerve-wracking experience less so; the opposite effect was seen as a result of a lack of rest, nutritional fuel, and exercise.

Benefits and Types of Exercise

We all know exercise has myriad benefits, including acting as a stress reliever for dogs and people. A dog who is anxious about being left alone will feel less acutely so when he is worn out than when he is left home by himself with an abundance of untapped nervous energy. A tired dog is also likely to be quieter and less destructive. *It is extremely important that you exercise your dog before leaving him alone*. But all exercise is not equal.

A long walk that allows for sniffing here and there is an excellent choice as it is physically tiring, and provides mental stimulation by engaging your dog's senses. If you live in an area where you can hike, even better. Walking and climbing through brush and foliage, sniffing out scents left by all sorts of fascinating critters is, for your dog, a trip through Doggy Disneyland. That fun-filled physical exertion and mental stimulation is likely to leave your dog worn out and feeling quite relaxed.

You might choose a more vigorous form of exercise, such as allowing your dog to run at the park or chase a ball in the back yard. Those activities will certainly wear him out. But because aerobic exercise releases adrenalin, it's best to leave at least twenty minutes between the time your dog finishes running and the time you leave the house so that his adrenalin levels can return to normal.

Exercise should be provided at other times as well. Below are some suggestions beyond walking, hiking, and romping in the yard:

Swimming If you're lucky enough to have a pool, assuming your dog likes the water, you've got the potential for a great aquatic workout. Dogs who don't know how to swim can be taught (although stocky, short-legged breeds such as Basset Hounds and English Bulldogs really aren't built for it). Swimming is excellent cardiovascular exercise, and is a good choice for arthritic dogs as well as those who find other weight-bearing forms of exercise too painful.

Road Work This umbrella term applies to any type of exercise where a dog runs along with a vehicle, most commonly a bicycle. An attachment lets the dog run safely behind the bike or alongside it, depending on the product design. In a related sport, urban mushing, dogs pull a person on a scooter or cart. It's great fun, not just for natural pullers such as northern breeds, but for any dog who's physically able and has the inclination. (See *Resources* for info on bicycle attachments and urban mushing.)

> If your dog has physical limitations or medical conditions, clear all exercise with your veterinarian. Even if your dog is in perfect health, ease him into an exercise program by building duration and exertion levels gradually.

Playtime with Other Dogs Forget the WWF—doggy wrestling is where it's at! When dogs spend time wrestling with their buddies, they are very likely to become pleasantly worn out. If they run around between rounds, even better. If you know anyone who has a dog yours enjoys wrestling with, set up play dates. You could switch off between your home and theirs, or meet at a local park during off hours.

A word about dog parks: while they can be useful in providing your dog with exercise, they are also often arenas for fights, and can create behavior problems where none existed; for example, a dog is attacked, which prompts him to become reactive toward unfamiliar dogs. (If your own dog is nervous or reactive around other dogs, skip dog parks altogether!) The safest way to make use of dog parks is to frequent them at off hours, such as very early in the morning when fewer dogs are present. You can also make new friends at the park and then arrange for private play dates.

If you do frequent dog parks, your dog should have a solid, reliable recall, meaning he'll come when you call even if he's running toward another dog. Use caution in assessing potential play buddies, and throughout your visit, remain alert and close to your dog so you can step in and break things up if play becomes too rough; it's all too easy for uninterrupted, rough play to escalate into aggression. Unfortunately, there are people who bring aggressive dogs to parks, thinking their behavior will improve solely through exposure to other dogs. You must be your dog's advocate. If *any* situation arises that makes you uncomfortable, take charge and put a stop to it. If necessary, take your dog and leave. Again, dog parks are not the safest place to provide your dog with exercise, but if you are going to partake, vigilance and a proactive attitude are paramount.

Chew Toys You might not think of chew toys as "exercise," but the right types of recreational chew items require exertion of the jaws and upper body. They have the added benefit of providing mental stimulation, which can be just as exhausting as physical exercise. (What tires you out more: thirty minutes of walking or thirty minutes of trying to balance a seriously unbalanced checkbook?) Best of all, chewing is a natural canine stress reliever. A well-stuffed Kong® (a hollow, snowman-shaped rubber toy with a big hole at the bottom and a small one at the top), for example, can keep your dog busy trying to excavate the tasty morsels buried inside for well over thirty minutes. By the time your dog is finished, he'll be ready to take a nap, or will at least feel more relaxed. (You can find Kong-stuffing recipes on the company's website—see *Resources*—and elsewhere on the internet via search engines. For a longer-lasting treat, create frozen Kongs.) Try other long-lasting chews too, such as bully sticks; it's all about what your dog likes, and what will keep him busy the longest.

Note: Avoid rawhide in its uncompressed form, as small pieces can become lodged in your dog's throat; also, some brands are treated with dangerous chemicals. Monitor your dog with any new type of chew item the first few times to ensure that he's not prone to breaking off and swallowing large pieces.

You'll be leaving your dog with something to chew on when you're away from home, so get busy experimenting to see what he likes, and how long the chewing fun normally lasts. For Sierra, the longest-lasting chew is a raw marrow knuckle bone (from a cow, obtained at the butcher). Some people prefer not to give their dogs raw bones, but if you choose to use them, follow safe handling procedures. Do your research, discuss it with your veterinarian, and make the choice that's right for you and your dog.

Interactive treat dispensers are another type of mentally stimulating toy that will keep your dog busy. The ones that are easiest to prepare and safest to leave your dog alone with are sturdy items made of hard plastic or rubber that your dog must maneuver to coax out treats. There are many to choose from, and new ones are constantly being invented.

Two of my favorite interactive toys are the Atomic Treat Ball™ (formerly known as the Molecuball™) and the Kong® Wobbler™. The first resembles a traditional ball but with large bumps; it's actually shaped like a giant molecule with a hole in it. Rolling the plastic ball around causes the treats to fall out. The latter is made of a harder plastic and is shaped like those old inflatable clown toys that pop back up when knocked down (fellow baby-boomers, sing it with me: *"Weebles wobble but they don't fall down"*). Thanks to a weighted bottom, the Wobbler lives up to its name. Your dog must use his nose and/or paws to knock it over so treats fall out of the small hole on its side. The toy then rights itself. The treat-dispensing feature, combined with the unpredictable way the Wobbler moves, has made it a hit at my house. Both toys are quick and easy to fill with dry treats. If your dog is fed dry kibble, you could place his entire meal inside, or just use one or more types of small, dry, healthy treats your dog likes.

Some of the more challenging interactive treat dispensers are actually puzzles with sliders that must be nudged and/or disks that must be spun or otherwise manipulated in order to reveal secret treat compartments. All of that problem solving will help to increase your dog's confidence levels while rewarding him for his efforts. Some toys, such as the Nina Ottosson puzzles (see *Resources*), are great for mental stimulation and confidence building, but are meant to be used only with supervision. Others can be left with your dog when he's alone. Test a few toys, find the ones you and your dog prefer, and then rotate them so he doesn't get bored with any particular one.

In my quest to boost Sierra's confidence level, I tried out a few different types and styles of toys, and we both had a blast. If you'd like to watch videos of Sierra testing out the Wobbler and other puzzle-solving toys, see the *Resources* section for website links.

Mojo excavating a Kong

Atomic Treat Ball

Nina Ottosson Dog Brick

Sierra tired out by the Wobbler

Again, I cannot impress upon you strongly enough the impact that giving your dog adequate exercise and mental stimulation will have on the success of your treatment program. Make a habit of taking your dog for a walk or hike first thing in the morning, or at least on a daily basis. Add in mental stimulation whenever possible, and *be sure your dog is always well tired out before you leave him alone*. Training, which will be discussed in the next chapter, is another form of mental stimulation that will help to expend some of your dog's energy.

Building Confidence

The definition of the word *confidence* is "the quality or state of being certain." Dogs who lack confidence are anything *but* certain, and may display a wide range of insecurities. Some feel nervous around new people or places, or are afraid of certain types of noises. Others are "globally fearful," and are sensitive to sound, motion, and touch. Unfortunately, many dogs who are insecure in general have a difficult time coping with isolation.

> A 2001 study found that dogs who had separation anxiety were more likely to have noise and thunderstorm phobias than were dogs without separation anxiety.[1]

Not all dogs who have separation anxiety have other obvious fears, and many seem like fairly confident dogs in most other regards. Still, it makes good sense to bolster the confidence of any dog.

Leadership

One vital element of the overall plan to promote self-assurance is to help your dog understand that you are a strong, capable leader on whom he can depend. Think about it: if you were someone who didn't like to be left alone, and looked to others for cues on what to do and how to behave, wouldn't you prefer to follow someone who exuded confidence and seemed to be in control, rather than someone who seemed a bit lost themselves?

Picture a person you regard as a strong leader. What qualities does he or she possess? Chances are the person is calm, decisive, fair, communicates clearly and directly, and is straightforward when it comes to what is expected of others. He or she inspires confidence and trust. You don't have to follow this person, but you certainly want to. This is the type of leader you should strive to be. If your dog knows you are in charge and have things under control, there is much less for him to worry about.

Below are a few suggestions for how to achieve leadership status in a gentle, positive manner.

1. *No physical force!* It's ironic that the more someone is a true leader, the less need there is for physical force. There is never any reason for you to use harsh physical means to discipline your dog. I have seen many well-meaning owners "punish" their dogs by forcing them on to their backs (the "alpha roll"), shaking or jerking them, or using other methods I won't even mention. Those actions are the attempts of a person who is not in charge to get control of their dog. Good leadership is not established by physical force.

That's not to say that your dog shouldn't have rules and boundaries—quite the contrary. If your dog is engaged in an activity you'd prefer he stop, a simple verbal interruption can be quite effective: a sharp, guttural, "Eh-eh!" is enough to startle most dogs out of what they're doing. If that doesn't work, try clapping your hands together sharply. Once your dog has stopped, calmly redirect him to another activity such as chewing on an appropriate item. (Ask for a sit first, so your dog understands he is being rewarded for the sit rather than for the inappropriate activity.)

A "house line," which is simply a leash with the loop cut off so it doesn't get caught on objects, will also allow you to peacefully interrupt unwanted behavior. Let's say you have a dog who jumps on the couch and refuses to get down. Instead of grabbing his collar and yanking (which is not only rough but might get you bit), you simply walk up, take hold of the end of the line, turn around, and walk away calmly while saying, "Off!" House lines offer control and help to avoid the use of physical force.

2. *Body Langage and Verbal Communication:* When delivering verbal cues, use a calm tone of voice, and keep it simple. Don't surround key

words with extraneous chatter. "Kippy, sit!" is a more decisive cue than, "Come on, Kippy! Sit down now!" If your dog does not respond to a verbal cue immediately (assuming it is one he understands and has practiced), count to 30 silently. If he complies during that time, reward him. The time between the cue and the response, known as *latency*, will grow shorter with practice. If your dog does not comply even after 30 seconds, a gentle consequence should follow. The consequence might involve you walking away and ignoring your dog for two minutes, withdrawing a potential reward (like the treat you were about to give, or the door closing when a walk was expected), or gently placing him into the requested position.

3. *Control the good stuff.* Just as parents control the resources children find valuable—access to cell phones, television, and games, for example—you should be in control of the things your dog values. Food is one of the most important resources, as it literally means life or death for your dog. Does your dog's food come from that magical round thing that always seems to be full, or does it come directly from you? Present a meal twice daily. If your dog hasn't finished after 15 minutes, remove what's left. He'll quickly learn that food disappears if he doesn't finish it in time.

"The good stuff" includes more than just food. Petting, toys, and going for walks, for example, are probably all things your dog values. The goal is for you to control access to all of those things. It's simple; just ask your dog to earn them. For example, before the door is opened to go for a walk, ask for a sit. Before you pet your dog, ask him to lie down, shake, flip pancakes—it really doesn't matter *what* behavior you ask for, so long as it's something your dog already knows how to do. Choose toys that are interactive, in that you are a crucial element of the festivities. A game of tug, for example, isn't much fun all alone. Ask your dog to sit or perform another known skill, and only then, start the game. When you're finished, put the toy away in a safe, inaccessible-to-dogs place.

You'll be glad to know that in addition to making your dog feel more secure, these suggestions have the added bonus of eliciting improved compliance with your requests, and better behavior in general.

Confidence Building Activities

There are ways to instill confidence that are fun for both dogs and people. Some pursuits have the added benefit of providing physical exercise, while others offer mental stimulation; some afford both. Following is an overview of a variety of activities that can help your fur-kid to become a more confident canine.

Training, using positive, gentle methods is one of the best things you can do for your dog. It not only enhances your relationship and strengthens the bonds of trust, but will also stimulate your dog cognitively. Clicker training in particular is excellent for this purpose. The most common type of clicker consists of a plastic box with a metal tab that, when pressed, makes a clicking sound. (If your dog is sound sensitive, use one of the softer clickers now available, or simply substitute a crisp verbal "Yes!" as a marker.) The click is used to mark the exact moment a dog is performing a desired behavior, or part of a behavior. Because each click is followed by a treat, dogs quickly learn to offer behaviors in hopes of earning a click.

"Free shaping" behaviors means rewarding for small increments, building toward a goal. For example, to teach your dog to go to his bed, you might first click for a glance toward the bed. Once your dog understands that a glance is what earns a click, he will likely begin glancing toward the bed and then looking expectantly at you for a treat. You might then wait it out, only clicking when he also takes a step toward the bed. Further clickable behaviors could include additional steps toward the bed, approaching the bed, standing on the bed, and so on, until you were finally clicking only for your dog standing on the bed with all four paws. And you didn't have to utter a sound—not even a whisper! Clicker training is a lot of fun for both dogs and people. It's fascinating to watch your dog figure things out, and you might just be happily surprised to discover the level of his abilities.

"Capturing" is another fun aspect of clicker training. It's easy—you don't have to do a thing but wait for your dog to do something you'd like to turn into a trick or behavior. Let's say your dog has a habit of stretching in a bowing motion every time he wakes from a nap. With your clicker and treats at the ready, the next time he wakes and bows, you click and treat. After a few repetitions, chances are your dog will begin to offer the behavior. You could then say, "Take a bow!" right before he begins. Very soon, you would have a dog who was bowing when asked. Clicker training is excellent for training tricks, but is also useful for teaching obedience skills. By the way, the clicker and treats get phased out, so don't worry that you'll have to have a clicker surgically implanted!

Clicker trained dogs are the polar opposite of dogs who are "shut down" and afraid to offer any behaviors at all—an all too common side effect of harsh training methods, or even the use of moderately coercive methods with a sensitive dog. Your training does not have to be of the clicker persuasion, though. In simple lure-reward training, a dog is lured into position with a treat, and then rewarded. For example, a sitting dog follows a food treat that is held near his nose so that his head moves down to the ground, followed by his body. The dog is then rewarded for lying down. Since most dogs are food motivated, the lure-reward method works efficiently and quickly, with no force or coercion needed. Done properly, treats are soon delivered on a schedule of random reinforcement (the same principle on which slot machines work) as well as replaced by real life rewards, so there's no need to be concerned that you'll end up with a dog who only works for treats.

Any simple, straightforward program of teaching your dog new skills in small, achievable steps, and then rewarding him with yummy food treats (or a short game with a toy, if he is more toy motivated), will go a long way toward building confidence. Practice in short three-to-five minute sessions throughout the day, and make a point of doing a session or two before you leave the house. Just don't do the session directly before leaving, as it could become a predictor of your departure.

There are many excellent books and DVDs on training techniques. Be sure to proceed gradually and use plenty of happy facial expressions, praise, and rewards. If you'd like some professional assistance, check out the Association of Pet Dog Trainers (APDT). (See *Resources* for books, DVDs, and organizations.)

Tricks: When I taught group classes, the difference in students' attitudes when they were teaching their dogs tricks versus training basic obedience skills always amazed me. It was almost as though with obedience, some owners felt a grim determination to get their dogs to comply—after all, this was serious, important stuff! When they'd move on to training tricks, though, it was as though a magical eraser had suddenly swept that somber attitude away. People were laughing and smiling as they taught their dogs to roll over, shake, or spin in a circle. The dogs seemed to be having more fun, too. The irony is that it's *all* tricks to dogs; they don't know that "down" is an obedience skill while "shake" is not. So lighten up and have fun with your dog! Teach tricks, but imbue *all* of your training with a joyful attitude. Take classes, or learn from books or DVDs.

Agility: Dog sports are an excellent way to increase your dog's self-assurance. In agility, handlers run a course with their dogs, directing them as they navigate a variety of "obstacles." Among other things, dogs are required to climb an A-frame, sail over jumps, run through a tunnel, and weave deftly through a series of upright poles. These skills take time to master, and they also require self-confidence. A good instructor will help your dog to learn at a rate that is comfortable for him. If your dog is not dog-friendly, or you feel that a class environment might be overwhelming, consider purchasing an at-home agility practice set. You and your dog can still have plenty of fun learning together. Of course, your dog must be in good physical condition to do agility. If you're not sure whether your dog should participate, check with your veterinarian.

K9 Nosework: If your dog has a habit of sniffing out the leftovers you placed on the kitchen counter, you can now put that amazing sense of smell to work in a new sport called K9 Nosework. It's similar to tracking in that dogs are encouraged to use their scenting abilities, but in this case, the scent object is hidden in one of a series of boxes. The dog quickly learns to ferret out which box holds the treats, which are then used as a reward. The game is made increasingly more difficult as the dog's abilities improve. There is something truly awe-inspiring about watching a dog engage his natural instincts, and K9 Nosework makes it fun and easy to do just that.

Rally: This sport is competitive obedience's kinder, gentler cousin. Together with their handlers, dogs maneuver through a course that is dotted with performance stations, each of which has a sign that tells the dog-owner team what to do at that particular juncture. Signs at novice level might simply ask for a sit, down, pivot, turn, change of pace, or a brief weave pattern. Advanced level skills require more complex combinations of maneuvers. Handlers are encouraged to talk to their dogs, which makes the sport more enjoyable and less stressful than traditional competitive obedience. Rally is open to both pure breeds and mixed breeds, and dogs of all ages. Physically challenged canines and humans are encouraged to participate, and exercise modifications are allowed where necessary. Rally builds confidence while providing plenty of fun. Try a beginner's class. If you and your dog enjoy it, you might even eventually choose to compete.

Other Dog Sports: There are plenty of dog sports that build confidence through the mastering of specific skills:

Tracking is great for dogs whose motto is "the nose knows," as they must follow a scent trail left by a person's steps. Tracking is normally done in a field or rural area, but urban tracking is becoming more popular. Old, young, mixed or pure breeds can take part. Even dogs who are not dog-friendly can track, as close contact with other dogs can be avoided.

Canine Musical Freestyle is all about dancing with your dog. It involves learning specific maneuvers that are then combined into a routine and performed to music. The sport teaches tricks and precision, while being extremely enjoyable. At competition level, owners and dogs even wear matching costumes! Even if you do it just for fun, what could be better than you and your dog dancing joyfully together?

Other canine sports include flyball, splash dog, and lure coursing. Check out a variety of sports and choose one that is a good fit for your dog's physical condition, energy level, breed, and temperament. For more information on dog sports, training, and organizations, see the *Resources* section.

1 Overall, KL; Dunham, AE; Frank, D. Frequency of nonspecific clinical signs in dogs with separation anxiety, thunderstorm phobia, and noise phobia, alone or in combination. *Journal of the American Veterinary Medical Association*. 2001; Aug 15;219(4):467-73.

7

Pharmacological Intervention

"I'm not going to put my dog on drugs!"
"I don't want my dog to be a zombie!"

I have heard these types of comments over the years from owners of dogs with major separation issues. The sad part is that as much as those folks loved their dogs and thought they were protecting them by avoiding drugs, the dogs were suffering greatly, and could have been greatly aided by pharmacological intervention. Now, I'm the last person to cavalierly suggest that a dog needs to be on drugs; it's not the right solution for every individual, and there are potential side effects with any type of medication. But the side effects of chronic, severe emotional distress must also be considered. Just as with people, constant or even frequent anxiety can cause all manner of physical ills. Dogs can become afflicted with gastric ulcers, atrophy of the lymphatic glands, and even suppression of the immune system, which in turn opens the door for illness and disease.

That said, a course of drug therapy, as helpful as it may be, is not likely to solve your dog's separation issues on its own. *Drugs are meant to be used in conjunction with a behavior modification program, not as an alternative to it.*

When are Drugs Appropriate?

Appropriate candidates for pharmacological intervention fall into two categories. In the first are those whose issues are so severe that they impact the dog's health or well being; for example, dogs who bloody themselves trying to claw or chew through doors to follow their owners, crash through windows, or self-mutilate when left in crates or other enclosed areas. On a less dramatic note, also included in this group are dogs who are not necessarily dramatic escape artists or self-destructive, but who become extremely overwrought, drooling, trembling, panting, and the like. Not only is the expression of the distress potentially disturbing to neighbors should the dog bark or howl excessively, but even without the vocalization aspect, again, the chronic stress can take a serious toll on the dog's health.

The second category of potential candidates for drug therapy consists of dogs whose human families are no longer willing or able to deal with the behavioral issues. While most people have compassion for dogs who are in distress, it can become difficult to remain sympathetic when returning home day after day to find damaged valuables, large-scale destruction, and urination and defecation everywhere. Feelings of frustration and hopelessness are quite understandable, especially if serious attempts at behavior modification are being made and non-pharmacological adjuncts have failed. Although many dogs can be rehabilitated without the use of drugs, for those who truly need it, medication, along with behavioral therapy, can make the difference between a dog having a loving "forever home," and being rehomed, surrendered to a shelter, or even euthanized. In short, pharmacological intervention is sometimes the kindest, most compassionate route.

When we first adopted Sierra, even though I was aware she'd been in the shelter four times in her short life and that she had a serious case of isolation distress, I resisted pharmacological intervention. Instead, I optimistically embarked on a program of intensive behavior modification. It was extremely challenging at times, and yet I firmly believed that if I could just stick with the program long enough, it would be successful. Perhaps this "natural" approach would have worked eventually, but my business travel schedule was creating a pressing need for timely success, and besides, the intensity of the issue had become glaringly apparent. Seven weeks in, tired and frustrated, I threw up my hands and cried, "One of us needs to be on drugs!" I chose Sierra.

It should be noted that there is absolutely nothing wrong with trying non-pharmacological interventions, and there are a variety of natural products that can be helpful for many dogs (see pp. 109-110). But if your dog's separation issue is severe, you must acknowledge his emotional state and provide him with effective relief as quickly as possible.

Which Drug is Which?

There are two main groups of drugs that are typically used in the long-term treatment of canine behavioral problems. The first, SSRIs (Selective Serotonin Reuptake Inhibitors), work by preventing the neurotransmitter serotonin from being reabsorbed by certain nerve cells in the brain, thereby allowing more serotonin to continue circulating. Higher levels of brain serotonin translate to a calmer dog. Drugs in this class include fluoxetine (Prozac, and more recently, Reconcile), paroxetine (Paxil), and sertraline (Zoloft).

In a double-blind study[1] involving 242 dogs and 35 veterinary clinics, dogs with separation anxiety who were treated with Reconcile in conjunction with a behavior program had a greater incidence of improvement as compared with dogs given a placebo along with a behavior program. In addition, approximately 42% of the dogs treated with Reconcile improved within 1 week of treatment, as opposed to 17% of the placebo-treated dogs. Both groups continued to improve over the eight-week treatment period, with an end result of 72% improvement in the Reconcile-treated dogs and 50% in the placebo-treated dogs, as reported by owners.

The second type of drug is TCAs, or Tricyclic Antidepressants. TCAs do what SSRIs do, but they also block the reabsorbtion of norepinephrine and, to a lesser extent, dopamine. Drugs included in this category are clomipramine (Clomicalm) and amitriptyline (Elavil). TCAs can have a bit more of a sedative effect than SSRIs. At the time of this printing, Clomicalm and Reconcile are the only two drugs approved by the FDA for the treatment of canine separation anxiety.

A study done in 2000[2] measured the effects of clomipramine in treating dogs who exhibited behavior that suggested hyperattachment to the owner, as well as at least one of the following signs in the owner's absence: destruction, defecation, urination and/or vocalization. During a three-month period, the dogs were evaluated at four times: days 0, 28, 56, and 84. The results showed that compared to the placebo group, the group that received a standard dose of clomipramine was rated improved at least three times faster for the destruction, urination, and defecation (all signs were improved except vocalization). In both this study and the Reconcile study, that results were seen so quickly might well have made the difference in the dogs' families being willing to continue working on a behavior modification program. Just as with any diet or exercise program, we are more motivated to continue on if we see early success.

> Medications can be costly. If your veterinarian prescribes a generic form of a drug, check whether it is available at your local Costco, Sam's Club, WalMart, or other large discount chain. You could end up paying less than half of what you would elsewhere.

Depending on the degree of your dog's anxiety, a short-acting drug may be prescribed along with the long-term medication. The addition might benefit your dog if, for example, he goes into a full-blown panic immediately upon your departure. In that type of scenario, waiting four to six weeks for a TCA or SSRI to kick in might not be an option. Benzodiazepines such as alprazolam (Xanax) or diazepam (Valium) are sometimes used for short-term intervention to lower canine anxiety levels quickly and safely. Because these drugs are not long-acting, they are normally administered an hour or so before the owner's departure, and are thought to last roughly six hours.

Both SSRIs and TCAs alter the neurochemistry of the canine brain so that overall mood is improved and stress levels are lessened. Dogs feel calmer and more relaxed when left alone, which in turn affords the opportunity to begin a behavior modification program with an increased potential for success.

It may be that a behavior modification program, with or without the assistance of medication, will show results within a few months. But a few months can be a long, painful time for both dogs and owners when a severe separation issue is involved. If drugs can speed the process by relaxing the dog enough that a behavior program can gain a foothold, it may well be worth pursuing.

Obtain a referral to a qualified canine behavior specialist (see *Resources* or ask around) to address the behavior modification portion of the program. However, this type of professional will not be able to prescribe medication, and should work in cooperation with your veterinarian.

Another professional from whom you could seek help is a board-certified veterinary behaviorist. This type of veterinarian specializes in behavior issues as well as having the authority to prescribe drugs. Many are available to work with you either directly or through your own veterinarian. See *Resources* for organizations that can refer you to a veterinary behaviorist.

The medication we used with Sierra was clomipramine. After only a week, her anxiety had noticeably lessened, which was a great relief. This is not to suggest that clomipramine or other drugs normally work this quickly, or that clomipramine is the right choice for your dog. Your veterinarian and/or a veterinary behaviorist should advise you as to which drug would be appropriate for your individual dog. Again, drugs alone will not solve this type of problem permanently, and keeping Sierra on clomipramine long-term was not something with which I would have felt comfortable; it might also have been medically unsafe.

You might be wondering why this discussion of pharmacological intervention appears even before the introduction of behavior modification protocols. Again, it's not because I am suggesting that your dog needs medication. But if, after careful consideration and consultation with a behavior specialist and your veterinarian, you determine that in your dog's case a course of drug therapy would useful, you'll want to start sooner rather than later. Depending on the drug, some effects may be seen as early as within a week, but it could take two to four weeks (or in some cases even longer) for the drug to build up sufficiently in your dog's system that significant results are seen. Based on your dog's reaction, your vet may need to raise or lower the dosage, or switch medications altogether.

Eventually, once the medication and behavior modification have done their jobs and your dog has become more comfortable being left alone, you will wean him very gradually, under veterinary supervision, off the drug. It's reasonable to assume that without adjunctive behavioral therapy, once your dog was weaned off the medication, the symptoms would return. Keeping your dog on a drug permanently to suppress symptoms of anxiety is *not* the answer, and could even prove dangerous.

Other Considerations

When assessing any type of potential pharmacological treatment, it is crucial that you take into consideration your dog's age and physical condition. Your veterinarian can advise you on those factors, and should also disclose any potential side effects so you can make an informed decision. If the subject doesn't come up, ask. The Merck Veterinary Manual online lists potential side effects of common canine medications. (See *Resources*.)

Regardless of which drug is prescribed, your veterinarian should draw blood before beginning therapy in order to obtain a baseline with which to compare future blood samples. Your dog should be retested periodically as long as he is on the medication to make sure he has not developed abnormally high levels of liver enzymes, or other physical problems.

While many dogs can be weaned off medication after a few months, how long the drug should be administered and at what dosage depends very much on your individual dog. Just remember that behavior modification, which we will discuss next, must be done hand in hand with any type of pharmacological intervention.

1 Simpson, B.S. et al.: Effects of Reconcile (Fluoxetine) Chewable Tablets Plus Behavior Management for Canine Separation Anxiety *Veterinary Therapeutics*, (Spring 2007) 1:8

2 King, J.N. et al.: Treatment of separation anxiety in dogs with clomipramine: results from a prospective, randomized, double-blind, placebo-controlled, parallel-group, multicenter clinical trial *Applied Animal Behaviour Science,* (April 2000) 67:4, (255-275)

PART III

Behavior Modification

Behavior Modification

This section contains step-by-step behavior modification protocols. Included are instructions for desensitizing your dog to *departure cues*—those things that alert him that you're preparing to leave—as well as desensitizing him to your absence in very small increments. The protocols can be extremely helpful in teaching your dog that the world does not come to an end when you walk out the door, and to remain calm during your absences.

There are, however, some situations in which these protocols may not be absolutely necessary. *If your dog's issues are mild* and you would prefer to hold off on working through the protocols for now, begin by implementing everything *but* the behavioral protocols. Read the upcoming chapters *The Alone Zone (Chapter 8)* and *Sleeping Arrangements and Gentle Disengagement (Chapter 9)*. In former, you'll choose a space where your dog can feel safe while you're away. The suggestions in the latter contain what may amount to some gentle lifestyle changes, so that your dog can better stand on his own four paws with confidence.

Also, to recap from previous chapters:

1. Use good management so that your dog is not left alone for longer than he is comfortable.
2. If necessary, upgrade to a better diet.
3. Give your dog more exercise, and be sure he's pleasantly tired out before your departures.
4. Implement good leadership skills.
5. Practice training daily.

…and as always, never use physical force.

In addition, if you are planning to skip the behavior protocols for now, turn directly to Part IV and read about the "Quartet of Cool Tools." Try each one alone and then in combination until you find the ones that are useful for your dog.

If your dog's issues are moderate to severe, the protocols should be implemented right away. Don't worry that these detailed plans will be overwhelming—they're not as complicated or time-consuming as you might think, and there's no completion deadline. Work through them at your own pace. Even if you remain at one step for a few weeks, that's perfectly fine.

If you are currently experiencing a stressful, busy period in your life and can't imagine how you'll be able to do even "one more thing," begin with the recommendations above for dogs with mild issues. Then, after a few weeks, evaluate your dog's progress. If the changes you made solved the problem, great! But if your dog needs further help, ease into the protocols a little bit at a time.

Next stop, *The Alone Zone*.

The Alone Zone

You may have heard that it's not a good idea to leave a dog who has separation anxiety crated. Or, you might have been told that an anxious dog *must* be confined to a crate in your absence, lest he destroy the house. The truth lies somewhere in between, because the appropriate solution depends on your particular dog. Wherever you choose to leave him, it must be somewhere your dog feels safe. Let's examine your options for an Alone Zone.

Crating

Crates can be excellent management tools for preventing dogs from destroying things when their people are away. If your dog is accustomed to and likes being in his crate, and his overall anxiety level is low to moderate, he might do well crated. I say *might* because simply being comfortable in a crate is not a clear predictor of a dog being calm in one when left alone; it just means it's an option.

Let's examine two different scenarios: Sasha, a five-year-old terrier mix, paces constantly from door to window and back when her owners are gone, periodically jumping up on the furniture to get a better view. During the first five minutes, she whines as she paces, and barks intermittently. But as time goes on her arousal levels steadily increase, fueled by the physical act of pacing. After fifteen minutes, she is barking in a way that suggests panic. It is possible that if Sasha had been comfortably crated, her initially low arousal levels would not have escalated to such a degree.

Trevor is a two-year-old Siberian Husky. Typical of the breed, he is a high-energy dog who requires plenty of exercise. Although Trevor's owner Doug understands Trevor's needs and provides for them, Trevor has a hard time settling down when left alone. Even after a three-mile run, he has plenty of energy to claw at the window frame after Doug has left. Crating might seem like the perfect solution as far as stopping the damage. But because Trevor is so worked up immediately after Doug's departure, he might well injure himself in an attempt to escape the crate.

If your dog's issue is severe—for example, he's intensely anxious with an obvious inability to settle, or is clawing himself bloody at doorways or trying to follow you by crashing through windows—do not use a crate. Dogs who experience an extreme level of anxiety when left alone are at risk for self-mutilation when left in small, confined spaces. They may also injure themselves in desperate attempts to escape. I have heard stories of dogs who have broken a paw or a leg, severely bloodied their mouth, and even broken teeth on either wire or plastic crates. If your dog experiences an extreme level of distress, your veterinarian can advise you regarding short-term drugs that will help immediately, as well as longer-term medications. For now, create a confinement space as described on the following pages or leave your dog loose, depending on which is more comfortable for him and is feasible given his behavioral tendencies.

If a crate seems to be a viable option but your dog is not accustomed to one, it's not too late. There are many books and DVDs that can help. One DVD that has a section specifically devoted to how to introduce and acclimate a dog to a crate is *Train Your Dog, The Positive Gentle Method* (see *Resources*); but any instructional source that teaches gradual, gentle crate acclimation will serve the purpose.

Some dogs do better in plastic crates, as they offer more of an enclosed feeling, while others prefer metal wire crates. My preference is the plastic crate. If you use a wire crate, be sure to use a pad or bed that blocks paws from getting stuck between the metal bars.

Don't worry if you're not sure at this point whether crating is an option for your dog. Since you'll be building "away time" in small increments, you will be able to judge whether the crate is a safe choice before leaving your dog in one for a long period.

Gating

Some dogs do better confined but with a bit more space than a crate affords. Good choices for a safe confinement space are your kitchen, laundry room, bedroom, or any other area that's large enough for your dog to walk back and forth a bit. If your dog is not housebroken, choose an area with flooring that will be easy to clean; a laundry room with linoleum tile is a better choice than a carpeted bedroom. If your dog is not likely to have potty accidents, consider that some dogs do better when confined to the bedroom, since they can lie on the bed or floor surrounded by their owner's scent. Just be sure to put away any valuables that your dog could destroy, as well as anything that is potentially hazardous.

The space must lend itself to having a gate placed across the entrance. A gate will allow your dog to see out, and will create the illusion of being less confined. You will also want your dog to be comfortable, so place his bed in the area, along with plenty of water. If you have a young puppy or a dog with special medical needs, provide an appropriate elimination area by placing absorbent pads or another type of potty product at the opposite end of the space from his resting area.

> Many people confine their dogs to the bathroom with the door closed, only to return to a room that's been festively redecorated in the classic Toilet Paper motif. Being unable to see out creates stress and frustration. If you choose to use the bathroom as your dog's Alone Zone, use a gate.

If you have a small dog, a single baby gate should do the trick. If your dog is likely to jump over a baby gate, stack one on top of another to create double the height. If he's the type that will climb a gate, here are two solutions: attach some shade cloth or other material to the inside of the gate so your dog's paws won't be able to gain purchase; or, use a wrought iron gate instead, which, by virtue of its vertical slatted design, is impossible to climb.

If the opening to your confinement area is larger than a typical doorway, or the space has an unusual layout, there's good news. A few companies now offer a wide variety of gate sizes and configurations. One is sure to serve your needs. (See *Resources*.) You could also opt to use a puppy pen (also known as an exercise pen or ex-pen), or even a small indoor kennel run, which is secure but still affords more space than a crate.

Another type of confinement space that some people choose is the garage. This is not one of my top choices, for a few reasons: first, the space looks and feels very enclosed to a dog, since he can't see out. Second, garages tend to get warm very quickly, making them dangerous in hot weather. And last, many things that are toxic to dogs, such as anti-freeze and paint, are often stored in garages. If, however, you have cleared away any potential dangers, the space is temperature controlled, and there is a dog door leading to a safe, enclosed yard, the garage could be an acceptable Alone Zone.

The Great Outdoors

If your dog does not do well with being confined, and yet allowing him free reign indoors is not possible because of destructive tendencies or other reasons, your best choice may be to leave him loose outdoors. Of course, that is only a feasible alternative if you have a safe, enclosed space such as a fenced back yard.

Some dogs who are distressed about being left will go to great lengths to try to follow their owners, so inspect your yard carefully for potential escape routes. When we brought Sierra home, the first thing she did was to walk very deliberately around the entire inner perimeter of our yard, checking the fencing along the bottom for ways to escape. I didn't like the way she was looking at the top of the fence, either. It wasn't hard to imagine how her particular combination of isolation distress and being an agile, intelligent escape artist had landed her in the shelter four times. Our fencing was already six-foot chain link, but I had a fencing professional extend it to eight feet and add lean-ins, which are the diagonally angled-in arms you see at zoos. That might sound like overkill, but I was adamant that this dog was not going to end up in the shelter ever again.

Walk the perimeter of your yard and inspect the fencing. If it's wooden, are there boards that have become weak and worn? If so, your dog could force or chew his way through. Replace or reinforce them. Are there areas that could easily be dug under? If so, be proactive: dig down a foot or two, drill small holes in the wood, and use sturdy wire to attach garden cloth (also called hardware cloth) to the wood. Do this all around the perimeter, making sure the metal sheeting extends in a few feet. Then cover it with tightly packed dirt and, preferably, pea gravel or another type of ground cover.

If you have chain link fencing and suspect it might not be high enough, extend it and/or add lean-ins. Wooden fencing too can be extended, with a bit of creativity. One option I particularly like is using "coyote rollers," which consist of a series of long, metal rolling pin type bars placed along the very top of a fence. They work by preventing dogs from gaining a foothold that would allow them to climb over. (Use an online search engine to find further information and products.) If you need professional assistance with containment, whether your fence is constructed of metal or wood, a fencing company should be able to help.

Note too the placement of garbage bins and other objects. If they are placed too close to a block wall or fence, chances are your dog can use them as springboards to jump up and over. Be sure gates are locked and, if you have gardeners, make arrangements to prevent them from inadvertently letting your dog out.

Clear your yard of items your dog could target for destruction. For example, pick up children's toys, and be sure the garden hose is safely out of reach. You will be leaving your dog with something yummy to chew on to engage his attention, but it's still best not to take chances.

If you just don't feel safe leaving your dog loose in the yard, either because of potential destruction or escape attempts, an outdoor kennel run could be the answer. Be sure the chain link dog run you purchase has a secure top (unless your dog is very small and unable to climb out) and a dig-proof bottom.

> Wherever you confine your dog, leave him with something that carries your scent. A soft article of clothing like a t-shirt or sweatshirt you've been wearing is best. A towel you've wiped on your body works too. When you're away, your scent will provide comfort.

Barrier Frustration

Some dogs, if left loose in the yard, will paw and scratch at the back door or dog door to get inside. Others, if left loose indoors with a closed dog door, will spend the entire time trying to get out to the yard. Dogs who have barrier frustration not only do *not* do well in a crate or other small, confined space, but they have a very low tolerance for being confined in any manner. If that describes your dog, assuming he is non-destructive and housebroken, being left at large with an open dog door may be your best solution, since it removes the issue of barriers entirely.

Harley's Story

Amber Burckhalter, owner of K-9 Coach in Atlanta, Georgia, relates the story of how she solved a case of separation anxiety by modifying a dog's Alone Zone:

Lauren had recently adopted Harley, a handsome two-year-old Beagle. His history included several failed placements due to separation anxiety that manifested itself with severe destruction to the home, vomiting, and diarrhea and urinating both in and out of a crate when left alone. While Lauren was totally committed to Harley, she was worried that he would never be safe alone at home. She was spending a fortune on daycare for Harley during the work week, and felt trapped at home on the weekends.

Our training staff began a heavy behavior modification program that included obedience work, crate training, desensitization, reconditioning, use of holistic therapies, and more. Success was moderate at best. We decided, after much discussion, to introduce a daily SSRI medication to Harley in addition to the intensive behavior modification. His vet prescribed a popular SSRI and within three weeks, Harley had a sudden seizure as a result of the new medication, and was immediately taken off it. Lauren did not want to try any others and was at her wit's end. I called a meeting with the training staff and Harley's primary trainer, Kat, suggested we try a dog door. I said, "We have nothing else, so why not?" Within one day of installing the dog door, all of Harley's symptoms were gone! He now lives medication-free, happily exploring both inside and outside all day long, and Lauren has her forever dog.

Note: The preceding story should not be interpreted as a warning that dogs who are put on SSRIs will have seizures. Although it is possible, your veterinarian can tell you about potential risks so that you can make an informed decision.

Your Turn

After considering various ways to confine your dog, which do you think might serve as a possible Alone Zone?

Here are two sample answers:

- *Ali is only mildly anxious, but is still destructive indoors. Since she's already accustomed to a crate, I'll use that.*

- *Bella isn't destructive, and doesn't urinate or defecate when we're gone, but she hates to be confined. Maybe being left loose in the house is an option.*

Below, jot down your initial thoughts. Don't worry if you're not sure; you'll be trying this out in a slow, careful manner before you ever leave for a significant period of time. And you can always change your confinement choices as needed.

____

____

____

____

____

____

____

Millie's Story

Valerie Pollard, CDBC

A few years ago I was called by Francine, who had recently adopted Millie, a three-year-old Pug. Millie had come from a home where the owners were there most of the time, and she was allowed the run of the house day and night. Unfortunately, the owners were moving and decided they couldn't take Millie to the new state they were moving to. So they placed her with a breed rescue, where Francine found her.

Francine was a professional single woman who lived in a third story apartment by herself. She was looking forward to companionship with Millie and wanted to give her a good home. Imagine her distress when she came home to find that Millie was literally climbing up her drapes (ripping them in the process); clawing at the doors; chewing holes in her couches; and generally going through obvious anxiety while Francine was at work. The final straw was when Millie escaped through one of the windows and was found balancing on a ledge on the third story! That's when Francine called me for help.

We discussed the situation on the phone and I explained how important it would be to design a new safe area for Millie to spend her time in, as she couldn't be allowed loose in the apartment anymore. We thought about having a run installed, but there really wasn't enough room. We considered using gates, but Millie, even with her short body, had learned to climb them as a pup. And she was too destructive to be left alone in any of the rooms. Francine finally decided that the best thing would be to purchase a crate, so we set up an appointment to begin teaching Millie that the crate would be a peaceful, calm place to be when Francine was gone.

A crate is not always the answer for all dogs by any means. Certain dogs will panic in a crate and may need a more open space to feel comfortable. It's important to look carefully at what a dog's behavior is telling you when making these decisions. It was going to be extremely important that this initial crate training go smoothly. Since Millie had never been crated, a bad experience could make the use of a crate unacceptable. I explained to Francine that she should set the crate up where she would like it to be and let Millie explore it should she choose to. Under no circumstances should she try and put Millie in the crate before our appointment. I also explained that it would be necessary for her to decide upon an alternate place to keep Millie while she was at work until our training was complete, as it is so vital that the dog not undergo any anxiety in her new safe place.

The day of the appointment finally arrived. Millie was shy and a bit nervous and as I sat down on the floor near the crate. She showed no interest in coming anywhere near it. I had some delicious pieces of food cut into tiny pieces—nice, smelly little bits of freeze-dried liver. I first put a piece on the floor about two feet from the crate. Millie went up and sniffed it, ate it, and looked around for more! The next few pieces gradually moved closer to the open door of the crate. Then there was a piece just inside the crate, and after that, one further inside. Millie would duck quickly in, grab the treat, and quickly back out. That was fine!

These exercises must be done to the tune of the dog's comfort level, so they get to make the decisions. The trainer simply watches and moves at the pace the dog sets. Next, several pieces of liver were thrown further back in the crate. Millie had realized that nothing bad was happening when she was ducking into the crate, so she felt comfortable standing in there long enough to eat the few pieces, then backing out. After several repetitions of this, she began turning around as she went in so that she was facing the door of the crate as she stood inside eating the treats. When she appeared just fine doing that, I opened and closed the door a couple of times as she was eating. She watched calmly, and I was careful to end up with the door open so she could walk out if she wanted. But Millie was smart! She was beginning to think, *Why should I walk out again and again when I just keep coming in to get more treats anyway?* So she began to stay inside the crate and wait for me to toss a few treats to where she stood. At that point, I actually had to call her to get her to come out again!

Next, I began to close the door again (but not fasten it, just hold it closed). I fed her a few pieces through the bars and then opened the door and called her out. I repeated this a few times, and then actually fastened the door shut, fed her through the bars, then opened it and called her out. At this point she was running into the crate as soon as she saw me begin the gesture of tossing a piece into the back.

Next, I fed her through the bars as we had been doing, then stood up, turned my back, and then turned right back again and fed her a bit more. Gradually, I added taking a step away (then returning immediately to feed her), taking three steps away, and so on. Between each little set of feedings I would open the door and let her out. However, she really didn't want to come out as she was enjoying this game, and that was fine. Before long I was walking out of the room, pausing, and then returning to give her a treat and let her out. You can see how this exercise gradually progresses to extending the time you are out of the room, very slowly of course and always being careful to watch the dog's behavior and make sure they are calm and enjoying the experience.

When I was able to walk out of the room and remain out of sight for ten seconds, I had Francine begin to work on the exercise. All went smoothly! Now it was just a matter of Francine continuing to work on the exercises and extending the amount of time Millie remained calm in her crate, then gradually adding in the sounds of leaving (such as keys, door opening, jacket being put on), always returning immediately at first to give a treat so that Millie realized that the triggers didn't always mean that Francine was leaving.

Francine had decided to day board Millie at a kennel until the she was ready to be left home alone, and this worked very well for the two of them. All in all, it took approximately a month before Francine was able to leave Millie in her crate while she went to work. Francine would return home for lunch to let Millie out and spend some time with her before leaving again. Eventually, she put a tall exercise pen around the open crate and Millie was able to stay all day and remain calm, playing with her chew toys and sleeping while Francine was gone. A real success story!

While Millie's story demonstrates how a crate can serve as a safe, comforting Alone Zone, the story that follows shows that sometimes, creating an alternative Alone Zone is the better solution.

Munson's Story Cathy Bruce, CPDT-KA

Munson, a black Cocker Spaniel, was adopted by John and Melana McClatchey in September 2009 from a Cocker Spaniel rescue. At the time, he was about one-and-half years of age. The rescue was not able to give the McClatcheys much information on his past history, except that he had spent some time prior to the adoption in a foster home where he was kept in a crate in a room with thirty-four other dogs almost 24/7.

When John and Melana brought Munson home they learned very quickly that he did not like being left alone in the house. The first week, Munson burst out of the crate and, in his distress, proceeded to destroy the house. He chewed up window moldings; blinds; curtains; a book; and, he knocked several pictures off a table. At the suggestion of the rescue organization, the McClatcheys purchased a sturdier crate and began the process of trying to help Munson feel better about being in it. They fed him in the crate and gave him treats and toys there as well. For the first few days he was willing to get in the crate, however, when they would return home the crate would be several feet from where they had left it, and it was turned 180 degrees. After a few weeks of this Munson would not come near the crate, and became more and more timid when John and Melana would leave for work.

It was at this point, three weeks into the adoption, that John and Melana sought out behavioral help. When I evaluated Munson for the first time in late September I found him to be a sweet and workable dog, but highly anxious when left alone, especially when crated. He had been spending approximately eight hours a day in his crate when the McClatcheys were at work, and clearly did not enjoy being left in there alone. Because his relationship with the McClatcheys was still very new and Munson was anxious, I immediately recommended some activities that John and

Melana could do to help build their relationship with Munson and keep his stress level low. These included calm, frequent walks, perhaps hiring a dog walker to break up the day, giving interactive toys such as peanut butter stuffed Kongs, and playing recall games in the house like Round Robin Recall (calling the dog from one person to another). It was also recommended that John do a lot of hand feeding with Munson to strengthen their relationship. The McClatcheys were advised to start using the highest value resources such as marrow bones for crated periods, and to positively reinforce Munson any time he chose to enter the crate on his own by tossing a treat in after him. All of these protocols helped to build Munson's confidence.

The McClatcheys also worked diligently on the weekends with Munson to leave him alone for very brief periods of time with something really fun to do, like work on a treat-stuffed toy, to show him that sometimes they went away for only a short period of time and sometimes for a longer period—this way Munson would not be able to predict the length of the departure.

Another strategy that was utilized was switching up the McClatcheys' morning "leave for work" routine. This had become predictable for Munson so they began to remove those predictive cues, for example, pulling out keys at times other than when they were actually leaving the house.

All of these training strategies helped with Munson's isolation anxiety, but unfortunately, were not helping with the crate training, so it was decided to change the criteria and set a goal that Munson could stay by himself calmly in the McClatcheys' bedroom while they were at work. The McClatcheys persevered with the training protocols. They also enrolled Munson in a Reactive Dog class because he displayed reactive behavior on walks, which had made it impossible for the walks to be calm. Munson made tremendous progress in the class. The couple also set him up for success at home by removing things he might be tempted to chew on and destroy if he became anxious, and replaced those things with interactive treat dispensers and stuffed Kongs. This gave Munson something to do, as well as creating positive associations with being left on his own.

After several months of continued work and the addition of a dog walker who came in during the week, the McClatcheys started videotaping Munson when they left the house. The results were great! Prior to the training, Munson would have destructively chewed, barked, and howled for over 30 minutes. Now after they left for work he might bark one or two times, and then within five minutes or so settle in, get quiet, and eventually take a nap. The McClatcheys are delighted that they now have a happy and relaxed dog when they leave the house.

9

Sleeping Arrangements and Gentle Disengagement

In the field of dog behavior, traditional "wisdom" sometimes persists regardless of whether it was valid in the first place. In regard to dogs with separation issues, two topics in particular tend to be troublesome: sleeping arrangements, and how much attention a dog should or should not receive from the owner.

Sleeping Arrangements

It used to be "common knowledge" that allowing your dog to sleep in your bed could cause a separation problem. But a 2001 study[1] of 200 dogs with separation anxiety found that "spoiling activities such as allowing the dog on the owner's bed...were not associated with separation anxiety," meaning they did not cause it. Other research has yielded the same findings.

Although letting your dog share your bed may not *cause* a separation problem, if your dog already has one, sleeping cuddled against you is not going to encourage him to feel secure on his own. But don't worry: you needn't kick your dog out of the bedroom altogether.

Your dog can share your nighttime resting area, but he must have his own sleeping space. If he is accustomed to a crate, place one next to your bed. If he is not used to being crated, you can teach him. (Refer back to "Millie's Story" in *Chapter 9* for step by step instructions, or watch the *Train Your Dog: The Positive, Gentle Method* DVD—see *Resources*.) However, if your dog is the type who absolutely panics in an enclosed area such as a crate, this is not the appropriate choice.

An alternative to crating your dog is to place a dog bed next to your own, and to teach your dog to sleep there. Of course, your dog will want to jump up next to you, especially if sleeping in your bed has become an ingrained habit. But just as you would place a young child back in his crib as many times as is necessary, you can do the same with your dog. When he jumps on your bed, say, "Eh-eh" and gently place him back on his own bed, then softly praise him for staying there.

If your dog will absolutely not remain on his own bed regardless of how much time and effort you put in, use a tether to attach him to your nightstand or a nearby piece of furniture so he is able to lie next to your bed but not climb onto it. A leash can be used as a tether (place the leash around the leg of furniture and slip the clip through the loop), or, if your dog is likely to chew the leash, use a steel-coated cable. (See *Resources*.) Note that the tether should only be attached to a flat buckle collar or a body harness; never use a tether with a choke chain, pinch collar, or any other equipment that could tighten or cause harm. A tether should only be used when you are present.

> You can increase the allure of your dog's bed or crate by adding an item with your scent, such as a T-shirt or sweatshirt. It can also be helpful to associate the sleeping area with things your dog enjoys. You could feed meals in your dog's crate, or give massages or tummy rubs while he's on his bed. Valued chew items can be given in either area. Also, be sure to reward your dog whenever he chooses to rest in his bed or crate by offering praise, attention, and sometimes, treats.

Over time, once your dog has become accustomed to sleeping in his own area, you can begin to move him gradually farther from your bed. Even if the crate or bed ends up just across the room, you are using those valuable nighttime hours to teach your dog to remain calm even when he is not in close physical contact with you.

If you truly hate the idea of even this much nocturnal separation, think about it this way: If your dog can't be at ease a few feet away from you, how is he ever going to learn to be calm when left alone in the house? Be strong for your dog's sake.

Gentle Disengagement

You may have heard that in order to teach your dog to feel secure on his own, you must withdraw your attention completely—to absolutely ignore him. I don't know about you, but I didn't get a dog so I could pretend he doesn't exist! I love giving Sierra tummy rubs, cuddles, and all sorts of attention. She loves it, too. To abruptly remove all of my attention would most likely cause her to wonder what she'd done wrong, and why I suddenly seemed not to like her any more. To abruptly decrease your level of attention might well *increase* your dog's anxiety, the opposite of the desired effect.

The majority of dogs with separation issues are hyperattached to their owners. They follow them from room to room, unwilling to let them out of their sight. They're like small, furry secret service men whispering into secret microphones, "She's on the move!" Small, incremental steps must be built to span the gap between that intense togetherness and your dog tolerating being left alone in the house.

If you have a small dog and tend to carry him around a lot, it's time to allow him to stand on his own four paws. Place him on the ground for short periods at first, and then for longer ones. If you tend to cuddle and talk to your dog constantly, you needn't stop, but dial it back a few notches so that the affection is still there, albeit in a slightly less intense way.

To ease your dog into being separated from you, we'll first teach him that it's okay to spend time in the house without being in close proximity to you. (If your dog is unable to handle even these casual separations, skip to Chapter 11 and begin with the step-by-step separation protocols instead.) Choose a time when your dog is pleasantly tired out, such as after a long walk. Place him in his crate, behind a gate, or on a tether. Remain close by as you watch television, read, or engage in another sedentary activity. Keep these sessions short at first, building to longer ones. With time and practice, as your dog remains calm, you should be able to walk around the room, and even disappear out of view now and then. Build distance gradually as well, and incorporate being behind closed doors for short periods now and then. Monitoring your dog's anxiety level and modifying your actions accordingly will allow him to remain calm as you slowly increase the difficulty in small steps.

Settle

To help your dog relax during those “on your own” periods, it can be helpful to teach him to “settle.” Unlike a formal down-stay that requires a specific physical position, settle is more of a state of mind; if the body is tranquil, the emotions will follow. The end result is that when you say, “Settle,” your dog will lie down in a comfortable position and relax.

To teach the skill, choose a time when your dog is pleasantly tired out. It is not necessary that your dog learn to settle in a particular spot, but it’s a good idea to practice in his Alone Zone as well as other areas. If you have a comfy dog bed, put it to use. The bed will become associated with relaxation, and if you eventually choose to teach “Go to your bed,” you will have laid the groundwork for your dog to feel at ease there.

Wait until your dog is lying calmly, then pet him in long, comforting strokes. Many dogs will sigh heavily as bodily tension is released. As your dog slips into that relaxed state, say, “Settle” in a soothing tone. After many practice sessions, start to say, “Settle” once your dog has lain down, *just* as he starts to roll over on a hip or turn on his side, or gives another sign that he is about to relax more deeply. Soon you can begin to say, “Settle” as your dog begins to lie down. Eventually, you’ll be able to say the word and your dog will lie down and settle.

The preceding is only one of a few ways the settle can be taught. For a description of how shape the skill, see *Help for Your Fearful Dog* in *Resources*. You can also capture the behavior by saying “Settle” in a soothing voice any time you happen to see your dog begin to do so.

Don’t expect your dog to remain lying calmly for an hour the first time! Only you know your dog’s energy and anxiety levels; if you only achieve a five-second settle the first time, that’s fine. Gradually work toward your dog remaining settled for a minute, and then for longer periods, with you close by. Practice the exercise in different areas of your home.

Work toward your dog settling with you at more of a distance, and eventually, with you out of the room altogether. Once you reach that point, practice “alone time” a few times daily, building up to longer periods. You may also incorporate settle into the upcoming protocols as is useful.

Departure Cues

What are Departure Cues?

What tips your dog off that you're getting ready to leave the house? Is it the act of putting on your shoes? Grabbing your purse or briefcase? Picking up your keys or cell phone? Dogs are perpetual, dedicated observers, especially when it comes to things that affect them. They are also masters of prognostication—they learn very quickly to predict one thing based on another. Just as your hand reaching for the cookie jar means a treat is imminent, your departure cues predict a period of isolation.

Many dogs learn to chain departure cues together. Suppose your morning routine consists of eating breakfast, showering, drying your hair, applying makeup, getting dressed, gathering work-related items, putting on your jacket, picking up your purse, grabbing your keys, and finally, leaving the house. If you do those things in the same order every day, your dog may begin to "backchain" the steps, meaning he'll realize that before you walk out the door, you pick up your keys; right before that, you pick up your purse; what leads to that is putting on your jacket. You get the idea. I've actually heard of a case where a dog backchained the owner's activities all the way to the alarm clock going off in the morning!

Desensitization

You'll know your dog is on to you when he reacts to a departure cue. When you put on your shoes, for example, he might begin to follow you from room to room with that "Don't leave me!" look. Once you've picked up your keys, he might start whining. The solution is to desensitize your dog to each cue so that it no longer causes anxiety. This is best accomplished by performing each individual cue multiple times throughout the day without it being attached to the departure sequence. For example, five to ten times a day, pick up your keys, put them down, and then go about your business. At other times, put your jacket on and take it off again. Grab your purse, and put it down immediately. You can even open the front door and then quickly close it again. Yes, your dog will think you've lost your mind! You may feel the same way at times. But what you'll notice in short order is that your dog no longer becomes anxious when you do those things—and that's the whole idea.

> There are many dogs who will not become nervous until the very last cue or two, such as the donning of the jacket or the grabbing of keys. If that is the case with your dog, there's no need to practice the portion of the departure routine leading up to those cues, since it doesn't cause anxiety.

Once your dog is no longer reacting to individual departure cues, it's time to start combining them. Let's say your normal routine includes putting on your jacket, grabbing your keys, and walking toward the door. Do those things, but don't leave the house—instead, wait a second or two, then walk away from the door, put the keys down, and remove the jacket. Practice various cue combinations throughout the day.

In addition to practicing desensitization, you can also switch your daily routine around so that cues do not always occur in the same order. For example, one day you dry your hair and then get dressed, but the next day, you dress first. Some days you pick up your keys and carry them around for a few minutes while you grab your jacket and gather your things, rather than picking the keys up right before you leave the house as you normally would.

> Because it is difficult to monitor your dog's stress levels carefully while you're distracted with other things, set up a camcorder first thing in the morning. Then go about your usual routine in as natural a way as possible, continuing right up until the time you walk out the door. When reviewing the footage, try to notice at what point your dog began to get nervous.

Your Cues

Below, write down the departure cues to which your dog reacts, in the order in which they are normally performed. Don't include opening the door or actually leaving, as those things are a trigger for most every dog with this type of issue; we'll address those in an upcoming protocol.

Next to each cue, write down your dog's reaction. For example, in the left hand column you listed "put on my work shoes." On the right side, you enter "begins to follow me around the house" or "starts pacing nervously." The more observant you are, the better you'll be able to help your dog.

Cue	Reaction
______________________	______________________
______________________	______________________
______________________	______________________
______________________	______________________
______________________	______________________
______________________	______________________
______________________	______________________
______________________	______________________

If you do not have even a single departure cue written down—in other words, you are quite sure, after reviewing the filmed footage, that your dog does not show any type of reaction until you are actually walking out the door—you do not need to practice desensitization to departure cues. Sierra, for example, is an unusual case in that although she doesn't like to be left alone, as long as she knows someone is in the house, she prefers to spend her time outdoors lying on the ramp outside the dog door. I can quietly prepare to leave and she never knows I'm planning to go until she hears the front door slam. There are many dogs who truly do not become distressed until their owner walks out the door. If your dog is one of them, again, you do not need to practice departure cues.

The amount of time you will have to spend desensitizing your dog to departure cues depends on your dog. Some dogs will barely notice a jacket being taken out of a closet after they've seen it put on and removed multiple times over the course of a few days. More sensitive dogs may take a week or two to become less reactive to certain cues. Be persistent, because your dog *will* eventually stop reacting to departure cues, both individually and in various combinations.

Next, we'll discuss how you can begin to wean your dog off your oh-so-comforting physical presence.

Out of Sight, Out of Mind?

If your dog is comfortable being physically and visually separated from you in your home—for example, he'll voluntarily lie on his bed in the foyer while you lounge on the living room couch watching television out of his line of vision—you can skip to the next chapter. If, however, you'd swear there was an invisible leash attaching your dog to your side, or he won't let you out of his sight, read on. Your behavior modification protocol starts here.

> The goal of all the exercises that follow is for your dog to remain calm throughout. Monitor your dog carefully for signs of stress, and if necessary, proceed more slowly.

Physical Separation

In *Chapter Eight*, you chose an Alone Zone in which to keep your dog when you're away. Perhaps you decided on a crate, or the kitchen or laundry room with a baby gate placed across the entrance. Those areas are all conducive to successfully implementing the exercises that follow. If your choice of an Alone Zone was the yard, and there is a sliding glass door leading to the house, that's fine too. But if you plan to leave your dog loose in the house when you're gone, use a gated area or crate (assuming he's comfortable being crated) for now.

Place your dog in the containment area along with a nice, comfy dog bed (or crate pad, as the case may be), and a soft item such as a T-shirt or towel that carries your scent. The scent item will be left with your dog when you do actual departures, as it will provide comfort. Using it now as well will prevent your dog from being able to discriminate later that you actually leave only when the scent item is present.

Scatter a few treats in the confinement area. Avoid using tiny, moist treats that can be virtually inhaled. Instead, use small morsels that will take at least a few seconds each to be chewed, such as raw baby carrots or dried chicken strips. Alternately, spread a little bit of peanut butter inside a hollowed out, sterilized bone. (I do not recommend sterilized bones for regular chewing, as they are so hard they can crack a dog's teeth.) Close the gate, sliding glass door, or crate door. Move a short distance away but remain in sight. How far you should go depends on your dog. If he normally becomes distressed even when you move just a foot or two away, sit on the floor or on a chair just outside the confinement area. If your dog is already comfortable with you sitting a few feet away, start there.

Note: If your dog is much more motivated by toys than treats, leave him with a super interesting, novel toy to play with instead.

Relax. Read, work on the computer, or engage in whatever other sedentary activity you'd like; just don't pay attention to your dog. Attention, by the way, means touching your dog, talking to him, or even looking at him. And yes, I know it's hard to ignore that adorable fur face! Some dogs will whine at first, or keep checking that their person is still there, but most will settle down to eating the treats fairly quickly.

Throughout the exercise, you will have to periodically get up to scatter more treats (or refill the peanut butter bone). The idea is to keep your dog cool and calm as he happily munches away with you nearby, so at first, keep those treats coming! He shouldn't be without them for more than a few seconds at a time. Later on, you'll build longer durations without treats present.

After a few minutes of practicing the exercise, calmly remove the gate and let your dog out. Don't make a fuss; just go about your business. Congratulations! You've successfully begun to teach your dog to cope with being separated from you physically.

> If you're worried about using treats because of health or weight issues, you can use your dog's regular kibble as treats. If his usual kibble doesn't excite him, measure out a portion of a meal and seal it overnight in a plastic bag, along with some hot dogs or chicken. In the morning, remove the hot dogs or chicken. The kibble will have soaked up the tempting odors, magically turning it from bland bowl filler into yummy treats! Use the delectable tidbits just as you would treats, and be sure to subtract the amount from his regular meal.

Repeat the sitting-within-view exercise a few times daily, and as your dog becomes able to handle it, sprinkle in some standing up, then sitting back down again. Try standing, stretching, then sitting. Take a few steps away and return. When your dog is ready, begin to move a bit farther away, but don't go so far that you're out of sight—that's the next step. As long as your dog remains calm, begin to add in longer periods between the restocking of treats. The trick is, as always, to extend the difficulty and duration of the exercise very gradually.

> Whenever you begin a new round of exercises, decrease the difficulty level a bit from where you left off. In other words, ease your dog back into it. That rule applies to all the exercises you'll be practicing, as it will set your dog up to succeed.

Visual Separation

Once you're sure your dog is capable of remaining calm when separated from you physically, it's time to move on to visual separations. With your dog in his Alone Zone, scatter some treats. Sit as you were before, nearby but still in sight. Now, stand up, walk calmly around a corner so you're out of sight for one second, then come right back into view. Be sure to move in a nonchalant manner, and don't look at your dog or talk to him during the exercise. If you were initially sitting, go sit down again.

Wait ten to fifteen seconds, restock treats if necessary, then repeat. See if you can stay out of sight this time for three seconds without your dog reacting nervously.

Don't extend the time too quickly. Even if you only build up to being out of sight for five seconds during the initial practice session, that's perfectly fine. As you increase the duration of "invisibility" periods, your dog may begin to vocalize. If he does so in a mild way (for example, a soft whine), utter a calm, "Hush!" from out of sight and continue the exercise. If he sounds as though he's truly distressed, though, you have pushed too far too fast. For the moment, come back into view but don't approach your dog. Stay in the area, but pretend to be busy with something else. Once he's calm, do one easy repetition and end the exercise on a good note.

> If your dog normally follows you into the bathroom, practice visual separations by closing the door after you. Keep the duration to only a few seconds at first, then add time in small increments. If even a closed door is too much separation for now, use a baby gate instead. (Obviously, the gate is only a viable option if you're the only one at home!)

Another way to practice visual separations is to employ a down-stay. If your dog doesn't yet know the skill, teach it to him (see *Resources*), and then practice it in various areas of the house including the Alone Zone. (For our purposes, your dog is not required to remain completely immoble during the down-stay, but is expected not to stand up and walk away.)

Once your dog has mastered the down-stay, put him in his Alone Zone and ask him to lie down and stay. Place a few treats directly in front of him so he can eat them while remaining in a lying position. Walk out of sight for a second or two, then return, treat once more, and release him from the down-stay. Note that you are offering a treat even though your dog may still have some left, since he complied with your request.

Practice increasing the time you are out of sight just as you would if your dog were not on a down-stay. The reason for incorporating the down-stay is that carrying out an assigned task will engage your dog's mind. Concentrating on what he's doing will give him something to focus on, rather than allowing him the opportunity to spiral out of control emotionally.

Vary the direction in which you walk off, so long as there is somewhere you can pop out of sight. When you've finished the entire session—which might last five minutes, or even less at the very beginning—let your dog out. Don't make a fuss over him. In fact, don't pay any attention to him for the first few minutes. Lengthening your visual departures in gradual increments will help your dog to become comfortable with you being out of sight, whether you employ a down-stay or not. See which method works better with your dog.

Staggering

No, I'm not suggesting that your next activity should involve large quantities of alcohol! What staggering means, whether you are working with physical distance or visual departures, is that you should begin to stagger the length of your absences. Instead of practicing in steadily increasing increments of one minute, 90 seconds, two minutes, and so on, a progression might look like this:

one minute
thirty seconds
forty-five seconds
twenty seconds

Staggering the duration will prevent your dog from anticipating that you'll be gone longer and longer each time. Continue to return periodically between absences to give treats, but know that there will be times when your dog has eaten the treats and none are left. Not only is that okay, but it is actually a goal for your dog to remain calm as the "between treats" period is extended a little bit at a time.

What's Next?

It can be difficult to judge progress when you are intimately involved with the behavior modification process on a day-to-day basis. Keep a written log of your physical and visual separations, and your dog's reactions. A log will help you to remember where you left off, and will allow you to see progress. Below is an example of what a few individual entries on a single day might look like when practicing physical separations:

Day	Activity	Duration	Dog's Reaction
Mon.	sitting a foot away	3, 6, 10, 7, 12, 10 sec.	a bit nervous around 12 second mark (stopped chewing treats)
Mon.	sitting a foot away	6, 9, 8, 12, 10 sec.	better, looked up but chewed the whole time
Mon.	sitting 2 feet away	7, 12, 10, 14, 12, 18 sec.	"gets" the game/not nervous

Notice that when the distance increased by a foot, the initial departure time lessened by a few seconds from where the last repetition left off. Any time one factor in a protocol increases in difficulty, another should be made easier so as not to push your dog over threshold, meaning not to overwhelm him to the point that he gets stressed.

Continue to build the duration of visual separations gradually until you can go and watch television or read in the next room as your dog remains contentedly in his confinement area. During these longer periods, use longer-lasting chews, or go back periodically to scatter more treats. Depending on your dog and the severity of the issue, reaching this point might take days, weeks, or even a month or two. Remember, the speed with which you work through these protocols is not important; making steady progress is.

Once you've accomplished calm visual separations with distance, you're ready for the next step: departures.

12

The Faux Go

At first you will be practicing very brief departures—in fact, you won't actually be going anywhere. Instead, you'll be teaching your dog that the door opening and you walking out is nothing to worry about.

Place your dog in his Alone Zone with his comfy bed/crate, scent item, and scattered treats. Go about these preparations in as calm and matter-of-fact a manner as possible. If you are nervous, your tension will transmit to your dog, so try to think of this as a fun game. Make your usual preparations for leaving: put on your jacket, pick up your purse and keys, and do whatever else you would normally do. By now, since you've been practicing desensitization to departure cues, your dog should not become upset by these actions.

> Use the best, yummiest treats you can find, but be aware that dogs who are extremely stressed will not eat. If your dog is simply not interested in food when you're absent, go about the rest of the program anyway. His anxiety levels should decrease quickly to the point that he can eat while you're away.

Out You Go

Following your normal departure routine, open the door through which you normally exit, walk out, and close the door behind you. Immediately walk back in again, take off your jacket, put down your purse and keys, and go sit down. *Hmm*, your dog will be thinking, *that was weird!* Allow him time to settle down again. Then, ten to fifteen seconds later, repeat the sequence, only this time, count to two and then reenter the house.

Just as with physical and visual separations, the goal is to increase the time you are gone in small increments. Stagger the duration of the absences so they don't increase in a straight line. For example, stay out for three seconds with the door closed, then five, two, seven, and finally, four seconds. Keep sessions short and don't push too far too fast. Be sure to scatter a few treats between repetitions as well so that your dog doesn't begin to associate the treat scattering only with you leaving. During the first round of departures, you might only build up to being gone for five seconds; that's perfectly fine. The idea is for your dog to never feel the sting of anxiety at all, but to remain in that calm, blissful, treat-induced haze, barely registering that you've left.

Once you can remain outside the door for ten seconds without your dog reacting, add in taking a few steps away. Factor the walking time in to the total away period. For example, once you've closed the door behind you, look at your watch, take a few steps, and then return so that you've re-entered the house fifteen seconds after leaving. Keep increasing the time gradually, and take care to stagger the durations. Remember when beginning a new set of repetitions to decrease the length of the first absence a bit from the "best time" of the previous round.

> Continue to give your dog treats and chew items when you are at home as well as when you are practicing separations, so they don't become a signal that you are leaving.

Subsequent Departure Cues

Where you live will now come into play. If you reside on the tenth floor of an apartment building, for example, once you've locked the door behind you and walked down the hallway, the next departure signal will be the sound of the elevator arriving. In that case, simply call for the elevator, but when it arrives, don't get in. Repeat numerous times. (Yes, your neighbors will love you for this.) You are desensitizing your dog to the elevator as a departure cue.

If you have a vehicle and a choice as to whether it is parked where your dog can see it or not, park it out of sight for now. That should make things a bit easier, as the act of watching you leave can be one of the most anxiety-provoking parts of the separation routine for your dog.

If your car is parked in a garage, carport, or other area within your dog's hearing range, the ignition turning over will be an indicator that you are leaving, as will the garage door opening. So—you guessed it—break the routine down into small increments. Begin to add to your departure sequence the act of walking to your vehicle, then returning immediately to the house. Once your dog is comfortable, the next step is to walk to your vehicle, open the door, shut the door without getting in, and then return. When your dog is ready, proceed to opening the vehicle door, getting in, and then closing the door behind you. Wait a moment, then exit the vehicle and return to the house.

Remember to put on your jacket, take your purse, or whatever else your normal departure routine entails each and every time you do a practice departure. Otherwise, your dog will be able to discriminate between a "faux go" and the real thing.

Don't rush it. Proceed to the next step only when your dog is completely comfortable with the previous one. When you feel it's time, get in your vehicle, close the door behind you, and turn on the ignition. Then turn it off again, get out, close the door behind you, and return to the house. As you feel your dog can handle it, begin to practice sitting with the engine idling for a few seconds.

If you have a garage door, the next step would be to start the ignition, raise the garage door, lower it again, and turn off the engine. If all of this is starting to sound like a lot of work, don't worry; it sounds more labor-intensive than it really is.

Once you've practiced sitting with the engine idling for a few seconds, add in driving forward a few feet, reversing and coming back, and then turning off the engine and going back inside. (And yes, at this point your neighbors will be wondering just how forgetful you really are. Say it with me: “I’m doing this for my dog!”) Build up gradually to driving out of sight and just sitting in the car, timing it so that your absences lengthen gradually, taking care to stagger the durations. If you live in an apartment building, take a short walk down the block and then return.

Your goal during this stage is to reach a “faux go” absence of fifteen minutes. Scattered treats, while useful for the early portions of the protocol, are not going to last long enough to be useful for this phase. Chewing provides stress relief for dogs, and it’s important that your dog has something longer lasting to chew on during lengthier absences. Once you’ve built up to being able to stay out of the house for three minutes or so, give your dog a chew item that will last for the length of your absence but not much longer. A thin, compressed rawhide chew or jerky breast strip might do the trick. A loosely stuffed Kong, or bits of treat or kibble in an interactive food toy are good choices too, as the amount of treats can be adjusted as you increase your time away.

~ * ~ * ~ * ~ * ~ * ~ * ~ * ~ * ~ * ~ * ~

Once your dog can remain relaxed with you remaining away from home for fifteen minutes, having incorporated the vehicle if applicable, proceed to the next chapter.

Take Your Leave

Move on to this step only when your dog is comfortable with a fifteen-minute absence, as outlined in the previous chapter.

It is now time to practice actual departures. If you have a camcorder, set it up before you go. Try to accomplish this without your dog noticing, so that the setting up of the camera doesn't become yet another signal that you are about to leave. Ignore your dog for fifteen minutes or so before you depart, and refrain from bidding him a fond farewell. If you feel you must say something, utter a casual, "See you soon."

Note: If you live in an apartment or other type of dwelling where the sound of your car driving away is *not* part of the departure sequence, ignore the following section regarding the vehicle, and instead practice increasing your away time.

The Getaway

Following your normal departure routine, get in your vehicle and pull out of sight. Drive to a convenient nearby location. For example, visit your local gas station, fill up, and then return. Or drive to a nearby bank machine and conduct a quick transaction. So long as you have already built up to fifteen-minute departures (and practiced them recently), this new type of outing should keep you away from home for roughly twenty minutes. Don't worry, you'll soon be able to do other more time-consuming errands. As always, progress will be made in a slow and steady manner.

Caution: Take care not to go places where your return may become delayed. Early on, when I was at the point where I could leave Sierra alone for roughly forty-five minutes, I got stuck in line at a local clothing store. The staff was short-handed, and a lone clerk was left to check out a long line of shoppers. When I saw that, I should have turned around and left, but I didn't. I really wanted those jeans! As a result, Sierra remained by herself for almost an hour and a quarter. It set our progress back. Had those new jeans not been so tight, I would have kicked myself!

When you return home, refrain from greeting your dog until he has settled down from doing the Happy Dance. It's fine to give a quick glance and a calm "Hey, buddy," but then go about your business. Better yet, go review the camcorder footage. If what you see indicates that your dog was very stressed, you stayed away too long. Go back to the duration that was successful, and build smaller increments from there. If you were not able to set up a camcorder, simply take stock of your dog's state. If he's still working on his yummy chew item and barely lifts an eyebrow at your return, hurray! But if he's heavily panting, greets you in a desperate, wild-eyed way, or shows other signs of having been distressed, you've pushed the envelope too far.

Experiment with feeding a meal right before you leave. Just as with people, that feeling of fullness can be very calming. Notice whether it makes a difference for your dog.

Scatter brief departures throughout the day, every day. If you have multiple errands to run that would require you to be gone longer than the duration with which your dog is already comfortable, do a few errands, then return home. After a short break, go out and do the rest. *It is important that you get out of the house for short periods each and every day.* When I was at this stage with Sierra, it seemed as though we'd just be making progress when inclement weather would hit. I don't mean a little drizzle; nooo, we had multi-day storms with heavy rain and wind. That might seem normal where you live, but here in southern California it's a big deal. Although I would have loved to have been curled up on the couch under a warm blanket with a nice cup of tea, out the door I went. I share this because there will surely be days when you wonder why you are going to all of this trouble. If you need a reminder, just look into those big, warm eyes that are always chock-full of unconditional love.

As your absences lengthen, leave your dog with a chew item that will last longer as well. At this stage you might use a bully stick (a.k.a. pizzle stick) or a Kong® that is tightly packed or frozen. If you're not sure how long a specific item will last, give one to your dog when you're at home, and time it.

Recovering the Chew Item—or Not

You may have noticed that I haven't recommended taking your dog's chew item away when you return. Although doing so would get the point across that being gone predicts "good stuff" and returning means the good stuff is gone, the practice can also create a resource guarding issue.

When I first practiced departures with Sierra, I took away her chew item each time I came home. In short order, my sweet girl, who would never guard a thing, was lowering her head over the chew bone in a way that made me distinctly uncomfortable. Had I continued down that path, her reaction might have progressed to a warning growl and worse, which would have created a whole other behavior problem to address. As it was, for a while she would not chew valued items right outside the back door as she used to, but would instead take them to a distance where she felt safe from Mom. It was a sad state of affairs. Fortunately, that situation has improved. But take heed: it's enough that your dog will associate your leaving with receiving something super-yummy. Don't chance creating a resource guarding issue by removing it when you return.

By continuing these graduated departures, you will eventually get to the point where you can stay away for much longer periods. Just remember that each time before you go, your dog should be exercised to the point that he's pleasantly tired out. On days when you plan to be gone longer than usual, increase his exertion if possible. And always be sure to leave him with a long-lasting, super-yummy chew item.

As each dog is an individual, and each person will be able to devote a different amount of practice time, there is no way to determine exactly how long each of these behavior modification stages will take. You might breeze through the steps in just a few weeks, or need to work on the program for a few months. In more serious cases, it could take six months to a year, or, in extreme cases, even longer to get to the point that your dog is truly comfortable being left alone.

Keep practicing here and there throughout the day, each and every day that you can, knowing that you will eventually be able to return to leading your life without worrying about your dog's stress levels—and yours—when you are away from home.

Boomer's Story Casey Lomonaco, KPA CTP

"Rewarding Behaviors, this is Casey. How may I help you?"

The unmistakable tiny voice of an elderly lady replied, "Can you help me and my dog? I am 92 years young and he is thirteen, deaf, and blind. Whenever I leave him at home alone, even for fifteen minutes, he has diarrhea, chews his paws until they're bloody, and barks constantly. The neighbors are angry and my landlord is threatening to evict us from our dwelling. Is he too old to learn? Am I?"

"You said you were 92 years old, correct? Well, you're in luck! 93 is the cut-off. You're the perfect age to train your dog!" I responded. Grace and Boomer became my new clients. She wrote notes to and baked cupcakes for her neighbors and landlord, explaining that she was trying to get Boomer professional help and requesting their patience as we implemented the protocols. Boomer was also incontinent. Grace indicated she would prefer not to use potty pads but was amenable to incorporating the use of a belly band (essentially a doggy diaper in the form of a band that wraps around the dog's pelvis/waist).

This case was an interesting challenge, to say the least. While I know many behavior professionals choose not to work with separation anxiety cases simply because they can be a challenge to treat and require commitment, dedication, and creative scheduling, this lady needed help desperately. Luckily, as this lady was retired, she had virtually unlimited time and enthusiasm for applying the protocol correctly. I thought the prognosis was guarded, but generally favorable provided she was willing to invest the time into the dog she obviously cared a great deal for.

Grace's ability to live with her dog and her ability to live independently were threatened by Boomer's behavior. Her family was pressuring her to rehome the dog and move into an assisted living facility. "He's all that keeps me waking up every morning," she said. That was all the positive reinforcement she needed; the reward for Grace's efforts would be continued independence and time with her best friend.

I didn't say anything, but as many of you may well know, there aren't a lot of families out there looking to adopt a 13 year-old, blind, deaf, mixed-breed dog with behavioral problems! If we couldn't make this work, the prognosis was not good for Grace *or* Boomer.

The dog had always displayed signs of mild separation anxiety, which had intensified as he lost his senses of hearing and sight. As he lost those senses, Boomer would frequently bump into furniture and even tumbled down the stairs a few times. The incidents would cause him pain, and created a general fear of walking around the house, wondering what coffee table or stairwell would "jump out and attack" him. He followed Grace around constantly when she was at home, a true "shadow dog."

The training plan had three key components: crate training, teaching Boomer scent cues to back away from things that might hurt him, and desensitizing him to gradually increasing lengths of absences.

The crate training was necessary so we could prevent Boomer from injuring himself when his owner was away while we focused on the other two aspects of the training plan. With the help of some puzzle toys, Boomer acclimated to the crate nicely, and would soon go into the crate on cue. Since he was both deaf and blind, we used a tactile cue (a light touch on his left thigh) as his cue to "crate up." A D.A.P. (Dog Appeasing Pheromone) (*author's note: see Chapter 14*) plug-in next to his crate was used as well to enhance Boomer's perception of the crate as a safe and calming place to relax.

My preferred training tool, the clicker, was out of the question for this dog who could not hear it. Instead, we used a vibration collar to teach Boomer that vibrations = treats.

Using this collar, we next taught Boomer a variation of "leave it," which meant "back away from this thing." Since Boomer could not see the furniture nor hear a verbal cue, we used rags scented with lavender essential oil diluted in distilled water as the cue to back away. Lavender oil was especially nice to use for this because it also has calming properties for dogs and people! Rags were tied to coffee table legs and other furniture items. We used a baby gate at the stairs because there was too high a chance for serious injury should he make a mistake. When a dog's physical safety is threatened, sometimes management really is the best option; this was definitely one of those cases.

Once we had these things in place, we began using the crate to gradually desensitize Boomer to Grace's absence. Since Boomer was limited without two of his senses, scent was the most powerful communication tool we had at our disposal. Grace was kind enough to donate her favorite blanket to become his new crate bed, and her scent seemed to comfort him.

Boomer was extremely food-motivated for a senior dog, and for about a month, got all of his kibble from a MannersMinder® (an automated treat/kibble dispenser)* in his crate with the door closed when Grace was out of the room. Food *only* happened when Grace was out of the room. The MannersMinder® is wonderful, as you can adjust the settings so that it automatically dispenses randomly during a designated time interval. This allowed us to gradually increase the criteria for distance in a way that was very easy for Grace to implement.

Absences started out very brief, just long enough for Grace to walk into the kitchen and grab a glass of water; the next exposure level was going to make a sandwich or going out to get the mail; then, doing a load of laundry, followed by taking a shower. I gave Grace these "real life references" for timing her separation exposures to make it easy for her to remember and apply. By the end of the month, Grace could go grocery shopping, have lunch with her daughter, or weed her garden while Boomer relaxed in his crate with the MannersMinder® inside.

*Author's note: see *Resources* for the MannersMinder®

Eventually, Boomer was allowed full run of the house again, with the exception of the gated off stairs. Although he had free reign, Grace often returned to find Boomer snoozing in his crate! And because he knew where the obstacles in his environment were by scent and was taught that avoiding them was reinforcing and kept him safe, he no longer had to rely on Grace to protect him from the furniture monsters.

Boomer and Grace are two of my most memorable clients. To know that I was able to be part of giving them more time together will always be a special memory for me. They remind me of everything that is wonderful about my job – creating hope where it was lost or too far off on the horizon, especially in "impossible" training situations like this.

~*~*~*~*~*~*~*~*~*~*~

The inclusion of a photo of Grace and Boomer was not possible, as Grace has since passed away and Casey did not have contact with her family. But Grace left a beautiful legacy. Even as she and Boomer aged and life became more challenging, she was willing to make every effort to keep her beloved friend by her side. They were able to spend their remaining time together.

PART IV

A Quartet of Cool Tools

A Quartet of Cool Tools

The process of resolving a separation issue can be slow going. Fortunately, there are some creative, non-invasive tools that can help to smooth the way. If the problem is mild, one of the solutions that follow might be just the thing to help your dog feel more secure when left solo; used alone or in combination with some of the others, it could solve the problem completely, or at least play an important role in your overall treatment plan. If the issue is moderate to severe, you might find that one particular tool, or a combination of two or three, is sufficient to give you a foot in the door so your behavior modification efforts can be more fruitful.

In addition to the "Cool Tools" that follow, there are other natural remedies that may also be helpful. Two nutraceutical ingredients that have shown promise are *L-Theanine* and *alpha-casozepine*. L-Theanine, an amino acid, has been shown to increase concentrations of GABA, an inhibitory neurotransmitter, and increase brain serotonin and dopamine.[1] It also increases production of alpha waves in the brain, which contributes to relaxation.[2] L-Theanine can be found in Anxitane®, a chewable tablet aimed at reducing anxiety, as well as Composure™ Liquid (which contains L-Theanine, alpha-casozepine, thiamin and lecithin).

In an open field trial designed and performed by two veterinary behaviorists (Drs. Valerie Dramard and Laurent Kern) and presented at the Animal Behavior Congress, Zoopsy (Marseille, 2005), of 32 dogs, two thirds showed significant improvement when treated with Anixtane®. There was a significant reduction in clinical signs associated with fear, and the majority of dogs responded by the second week. The manufacturer recommends the formula for anxious pets and recommends that it be given for at least 60 days to ensure maximum results.

Alpha-casozepine is a peptide derived from a protein found in milk. This string of amino acids binds to the same receptors in the brain that benzodiazapenes act upon (without the side effects), producing a temporary calming effect. A 56-day trial[3] involving 38 dogs compared the effects of alpha-casozepine on anxious dogs with those of a control molecule, selegeline (Anipryl). Both were efficient to decrease the EDED score (a scale that assesses basic behaviors as well as organic signs), and owner assessment was also perfectly equivalent. In the U.S., alpha-casozepine can be found in De-Stress™ (Biotics Research), and in the U.K., in Zylkene®.

I tried Zylkene® for Sierra, and I'm happy to report that after only four days, the milky powder had obviously made a difference. Although she had been on a low dose of clomipramine for a few months and had made progress behaviorally, she would still be panting whenever my husband and I were gone longer than two hours or so. With the combination of clomipramine and alpha-casozepine there was no panting at all, even on the rare occasions that we had to be away for three or four hours. (Check with your veterinarian as to what is safe for your dog.)

All four of the Cool Tools that follow are relatively inexpensive, simple to use, and do not have worrisome side effects. They have helped many of my training clients' dogs, and my hope is that they will do the same for yours. At the very least, they fall into the "can't hurt, might help" category. I suggest you try each one individually for a long enough period that you can realistically assess whether it has had an effect on your dog's stress levels. You might end up adding just one to your overall treatment plan, or using a combination of two, three, or even all four.

1 Nathan et al. (2006) The Neuropharmacology of L-Theanine (N-Ethyl-L-Glutamine): A Possible Neuroprotective and Cognitive Enhancing Agent. Journal of Herbal Pharmacology, Vol. 6(2), 21-30.

2 Song CH et al. (2003) Effects of theanine on the release of brain alpha waves in adult males. Korean J. Nutrition 36, 918-923

3 Beata, Claude et. al. (2007) Effects of alpha-casozepine (Zylkene) versus selegiline hydrochloride (Selgian, Anipryl) on anxiety disorders in dogs. *Journal of Veterinary Behavior,* Vol. 2 (5), 175-183

14

D.A.P.

What is D.A.P.?

No, it doesn't stand for Double Anchovy Pizza—although considering some of the stinky things dogs roll in, that would probably make them pretty darned happy! D.A.P. is actually an acronym for Dog Appeasing Pheromone. Sounds like an exotic perfume for dogs, doesn't it? *Poodles, just a little dab behind those petite, furry ears and that handsome Rottweiler will be eating out of your paw!* Okay, maybe it's not quite *that* exciting, but the truth is still pretty intriguing.

Within three to five days of giving birth, lactating female dogs produce pheromones that convey a sense of security to the pups. Puppies detect the pheromones through the vomero-nasal organ. This sensitive piece of canine anatomy is directly linked to the limbic system, the part of the brain associated with moods and emotions. Through that connection, molecules of scent can actually affect emotion, and thereby change behavior in times of anxiety. (Scent is linked with emotion in humans too, as you know if you've ever felt a pang when catching a whiff of cologne worn by a former flame, or suddenly felt comforted by the scent of a favorite childhood dish.)

Dog Appeasing Pheromone products provide a synthetic copy of their natural counterpart by chemically mimicking the pheromones given off by lactating female dogs. Because those pheromones are calming to both puppies and adult dogs, the products are useful regardless of a dog's age.

Product Types

The most common type of D.A.P. product resembles and works like a plug-in air freshener. The electrically heated diffuser releases scent molecules into the air. Simply leave it plugged in 24 hours a day with the windows closed, in the area of the house your dog frequents the most. One diffuser covers roughly 650 square feet and lasts about a month, and refills are available. Oh, and don't worry—you won't smell a thing. If you have other dogs at home, the scent won't harm them, and they might get some bonus calming as well.

> D.A.P. products are not known to affect cats either way. If you have birds, however, do not use these products in the area where they are kept, as birds can be very sensitive to air quality issues.

D.A.P. also comes in a spray form, which is handy for misting your dog's bed at home or when traveling. You can also spray it in the car so your dog remains calm while waiting for you to run errands. You could even apply it to a bandana and place it around your dog's neck. The other around-the-neck option is the D.A.P. collar, which consists of a plain nylon collar featuring a small canister that emits the pheromone.

Research

There have been many studies on D.A.P. Here are a few findings:

- In clinical trials coordinated by French scientist Dr. Patrick Pageat, 11 investigators working in four different countries studied 26 dogs that displayed problem behaviors when left alone. Twenty displayed destructive behavior; 18, excessive vocalization; and 12 house-soiled. In each case the pheromone was emitted by way of the diffuser, which was placed in the room where the dog spent the most time during the day.

  By the end of the first week, destructive behavior was down 27 percent, and by the 28th day, the dogs showed an 85 percent level of improvement. Vocalization incidents decreased by almost a quarter in the first week, and after 28 days, there was an overall decrease of 72 percent. House soiling incidents were reduced dramatically by half by the second week of the trial, and after 28 days, had further reduced to 66 percent. Overall, at the end of the 28-day trial, 85 percent of the dogs were confirmed as cured or improved.[1]

- A 2005 study examined sixty-seven dogs who displayed signs of distress—excessive vocalization, house soiling, and destructiveness—when separated from their owners. These dogs also showed hyperattachment when the owners were present. The randomized, blind trial was designed to compare the efficacy of Dog Appeasing Pheromone with that of clomipramine to treat separation anxiety. (You may remember that clomipramine is the generic form of Clomicalm, an anti-anxiety medication often prescribed by veterinarians in the treatment of separation issues.)

  The dogs were broken into two groups: one received the clomipramine, and the other was exposed to D.A.P. The behaviors decreased in both groups, but interestingly, based on the results reported by owners, there was no significant difference between the two treatments.[2] In fact, there were fewer undesirable events in the dogs treated with the pheromone, and the administration was more convenient. That makes a good argument for trying this type of product before resorting to drug therapy.

- Another study compared the behavior of adult dogs housed in a public animal shelter before and after D.A.P. was administered. After seven days, there were significant differences in resting, barking and sniffing frequency (remember, sniffing is a stress signal) in response to a friendly stranger, with the D.A.P. treated dogs showing less stress.[3]

I have seen more dogs who have been helped by this pheromone treatment than dogs for whom the product had no effect, but there are those who show no visible improvement. In most of my clients' cases where it has helped, the results were subtle but noticeable; in a few, the results were more dramatic, as in the story that follows.

Enzo and Aldo's Story Nicole Wilde, CPDT-KA

Maggie Stone had a husband, two children, and two Italian greyhound puppies she'd obtained at the age of eight weeks. Now four months old, brothers Enzo and Aldo had never been separated, even momentarily. They played together, ate together, and even slept in the same crate. The problem with this scenario is that it creates a strong likelihood that when the pups would eventually be required to be out of each other's company, it would be extremely difficult for them to cope.

One of the suggestions I made was to physically separate the brothers at night by giving each his own crate. So as not to traumatize the pups, we would begin with the crates right next to each other. Over time, we'd move them farther apart.

I returned seven days after the initial appointment to find a family who looked as though they hadn't slept in a week—and they hadn't! Apparently, the pups had whined, barked, and even screamed when placed in separate crates, and they continued to vocalize their distress throughout the night. I suggested a D.A.P. diffuser, which the daughter immediately went out to purchase.

Maggie called me the following day to report that the previous night had been the first one where the family had been able to sleep. The pups had done their normal vocalizing routine, but after five minutes, had settled down and slept. The family was relieved. Of course, results certainly won't be this dramatic for all dogs, but it can happen.

If you choose to try D.A.P., set up your camcorder at the start and then again two weeks or so after it has been in use, so that you can gauge whether your dog's home alone behavior has changed. You may discover less pacing, barking, whining, and other distress signals and more calm, resting behavior. Or, the results may be subtler, such as decreased panting and less frantic greetings than usual upon your return.

You may be wondering how long it takes to see results after you plug in the diffuser, spray the bedding, or attach the collar. In my experience, some dogs respond as quickly as the same day, while for others, it can take a week to two weeks. As with so many other solutions, success depends on the individual dog and the severity of the issue. Although in some milder cases the pheromone treatment alone may solve a separation issue, in most cases it is more likely to serve as a useful adjunct to a behavior modification program.

Products containing D.A.P. are sold under various names and are available through veterinarians and pet supply retailers. (See *Resources*.)

1 Mills, D. (2002) *Veterinary Times Magazine*, October

2 Comparison of the efficacy of a synthetic dog-appeasing pheromone with clomipramine for the treatment of separation-related disorders in dogs. E. Gaultier, DVM, MSc, L. Bonnafous, DVM, L. Bougrat, MSc, C. Lafont, MSc and P. Pageat, DVM, PhD, CD, DipECVBM. *The Veterinary Record* 156:533 (2005) British Veterinary Association.

3 Tod, E., D. Brander and N. Waran. Efficacy of Dog Appeasing Pheromone in Reducing Stress & Fear Related Behavior in Shelter Dogs. *Applied Animal Behaviour Science*, 93:3 (295-308)

15

Music to My Ears

Music has the power to transform. It can lift our spirits, soothe us when we're frazzled, and cause such feelings of joy that our bodies can't help but move right along with it. And music truly is the universal language. The ebb and flow of sonic vibrations affects not only people, but also animals, and even plants.

In both dogs and humans, the nervous system is influenced by the tones, rhythms, and patterns in music. If you've ever bobbed your head or tapped your foot in time with a song, you've experienced *entrainment*, whereby your internal pulses become synchronized with the periodic rhythm of the beat. Through the musical entrainment of brain waves, heartbeat, and breath, bodily rhythms alter, which in turn affects mood, emotions, and behavior.

From Vivaldi to Metallica

In 2002, Ireland-based psychologist/animal behaviorist Dr. Deborah Wells studied the influence of various types of auditory stimulation on dogs. Fifty shelter dogs were exposed to five types of sonic input: human conversation, silence, classical music (including Beethoven, Vivaldi, and Grieg), heavy metal (Metallica), and a compilation of pop music that included Britney Spears and Bob Marley (one day someone is going to have to explain that last pairing to me!).

Dr. Wells' plan was to assess signs of relaxation in the dogs as they were exposed to each type of sonic input. More time spent resting, and less time barking and/or pacing, would mean the dogs were feeling less stressed. As it turned out, the dogs were indifferent to human voices, silence, and pop music. The effects of heavy metal music surely would have made the Metallica boys proud. Rottweilers pumped fisted paws in the air, while Afghans were seen tossing their long locks to and fro while howling out the lyrics. Okay, maybe not, but it did cause definite signs of agitation, including more barking than with any other type of auditory stimulation. Classical music, however, had the opposite effect: the dogs were quieter, spent more time resting, and appeared to be more relaxed overall.[1]

Through a Dog's Ear

Many people leave music playing while they're away, hoping it will make their dogs less anxious. Lisa Spector, classically trained concert pianist and dog lover, took it a step further. She wanted a music CD to sell at her northern California pet shop that would help to calm dogs, so she turned to psychoacoustics expert Joshua Leeds. Leeds teamed up with veterinarian Susan Wagner, and the duo conducted two pilot studies involving 150 dogs. The goal was to determine which types of classical music would most effectively cause dogs to relax.

After experimenting with different formats, Leeds and Wagner discovered that piano music alone was more successful than complex music with heavier instrumentation. In a home environment, the solo piano played at 50-60 beats per minute caused an average of 85% of dogs to become calm—in fact, over half went to sleep! (If cats were present they either stayed in the room or left, but at least they didn't become agitated or start critiquing the music.) Even in a kennel environment, 70% of the dogs became calmer with both solo piano and a trio of pianos at 50-60 beats per minute. The ideal human resting heart rate is 50-70 beats per minute. Leeds and Wagner had discovered that dogs responded best to the tempo that was also optimal for people.

The second experiment involved dogs with anxiety stemming from various sources that included, among others, separation anxiety. A non-psychoacoustic control CD was used along with the psychoacoustically designed music for comparative purposes. Results showed that "70 percent of anxiety behaviors were reduced with psychoacoustically designed music, while 36 percent of anxiety behaviors were reduced with the non-psychoacoustic control CD."[2] Although the dogs did become calmer and lay resting with both CDs, the slower tempo and simpler arrangements of the psychoacoustically designed music helped the dogs to relax even more. The product is available as a series of CDs called *Through a Dog's Ear* (see *Resources*).

Tips

Whether you use the aforementioned product or choose to play other slow, simple, classical music, keep the following in mind:

1. Turn the music on roughly fifteen to twenty minutes before you are ready to leave. Just as you would offer your dog a stuffed chew bone in advance of your departure so he can attain a state of chewing bliss, you'll want to give your dog time to relax into the music before you walk out the door.

2. Set an MP3 player or the CD to repeat mode, or stock your CD player with a series of calming music, but insert periods of silence as well so that the music is not constantly playing during your absence. Be sure the volume is low, as canine ears are very sensitive. Do not attempt to play the music loud enough to mask outside noise; if it's too loud for you to listen to, it's much too loud for your dog.

3. Be careful that you don't only play the music when you are leaving. If you do, it could become associated with your absences and actually make your dog more nervous.

4. Strengthen the association between specific musical compositions and relaxation by letting them play while you massage your dog, or while you engage in long, calming petting sessions or anything else that makes your dog feel relaxed.

Will calming music alone solve your dog's problem? Yes. No. Maybe. Of course, the answer depends on your particular dog. In some cases, music therapy is enough to keep a dog with a mild separation issue calm when left alone. At the least, it's another tool in your toolbox. And who knows, it might just make you feel calmer as well.

1 Wells, D.L.; Graham, L.; Hepper, P.G., The influence of auditory stimulation on the behaviour of dogs housed in a rescue shelter. *Animal Welfare*, Volume 11, Number 4, November 2002 , pp. 385-393(9)

2 J. Leeds & S. Wagner, *Through a Dog's Ear*, Sounds True: Boulder, CO, 2008

16

Flower Essences

Concept and Development

Plants have been used for healing throughout history, and the tradition continues. Many of our modern pain-relievers and anti-inflammatory medications are derived from plants. Aspirin, for example, is derived from the stems of *Spiraea ulmaria*. Morphine and codeine, two extremely potent painkillers, are extracted from the unripe seed capsules of the opium poppy. Although all parts of plants have been used for healing, flowers are considered to embody the essential character of the plant, and to have specific healing powers.

Healing with flower essences is based on the concept that everything in the universe has a specific vibration. When a flower is processed into an essence and that essence is taken into the body as a tincture, the body begins to vibrate at the same frequency as the flower. As the body's cells and tissues vibrate at that frequency, healing begins on both the physical and emotional planes. In short, the flower essence changes the energy of the body so that healing can take place.

In 1930, British physician and homeopath Edward Bach developed the first modern therapeutic system using flower essences. Bach believed in treating the cause of an illness rather than simply masking the symptoms, and that the underlying cause could be traced to a distortion of the body's energy field. He concluded that a positive, healthy state of mind could be restored by utilizing the energies found in plants, trees, bushes, and special waters. Bach identified 38 essences, each with its own specific purpose. The essences were divided into seven groups, each representing fundamental conflicts. Two of those groups are "Uncertainty" and "Fear," two emotions that are certainly facets of separation issues. The "Bach Flower Essences" were originally created for humans, but are now commonly used for dogs. They are widely available in liquid form at health food stores and via mail order.

Rescue® Remedy

Rescue® Remedy, the Bach Flower Essence that is most often used for dogs, is actually a combination of five essences. It contains Impatiens (for mental stress and tension), Clematis (for disorientation), Rock Rose (for terror and panic), Cherry Plum (for desperation), and Star of Bethlehem (for shock). The five-essence combination is used to ease stress and anxiety, which allows the body to achieve relaxation. The same combination of essences is sold by other manufacturers under the brand names Calming Essence and Five Flower Formula (see *Resources*).

Years ago, I worked at a doggy daycare center where 30 to 40 dogs romped together off-leash daily. For the most part, it was a fun experience for both the dogs and the staff. But some dogs were anxious because their owners were absent, others did not want to be bothered, and fights sometimes occurred. The staff always kept Rescue® Remedy on hand. It often helped to calm the dogs—and us.

Individual Essences

Here are some individual essences that may be used either alone or in combination to address separation distress and related issues:

Star of Bethlehem: Appropriate for dogs with a difficult past. Dogs who have been abandoned, neglected, or abused fall into this category, as do some dogs who have been rehomed.

Walnut: Addresses difficulty in adapting to unfamiliar circumstances, such as coming into a new home or someone leaving the home. Builds emotional independence.

Honeysuckle: An important remedy in cases where a dog is simply "blue" when left alone, or is pining for his owner. A typical expression would be lethargy without eating, or mournful howling. (If your dog is lethargic in general, however, a vet exam is in order.) Honeysuckle is also suitable for dogs who need to recover from the loss of a companion, whether human or canine, and can be combined with Walnut for assistance in adjusting to changes of home or owner.

Heather: In the words of Dr. Bach, Heather is for "those who are always seeking the companionship of anyone who may be available…they are very unhappy if they have to be left alone for any length of time." This makes Heather an excellent choice for dogs who have isolation distress, and can help to reduce the mental stress a dog experiences when left alone.

Chicory: An important remedy for dogs with separation issues. Particularly good for dogs who are clingy, won't let owners out of their sight (the follow-you-into-the-bathroom dogs), or display constant attention-seeking behaviors. Also good for those who are destructive or vocal when left by themselves. (In cases where there is a co-dependent relationship between dog and owner, both should take the remedy.)

Chicory is also an appropriate choice for dogs who show physical symptoms such as vomiting, diarrhea, increased heartbeat and respiration (you come home to find the dog panting and wild-eyed), or repetitive, obsessive behaviors, such as cases where the home alone dog displays excessive licking, fur chewing, or chewing on paws or other body parts. (Again, if your dog displays physical symptoms, a veterinary exam is in order.) For those with repetitive, obsessive type behaviors, Chicory can be combined with Rescue® Remedy and White Chestnut.

Rock Rose: Another essence that is part of the Rescue® Remedy formula, Rock Rose is for terror or panic. These are the dogs who are so phobic about being left alone that they try to claw through doors, burst through windows, or injure themselves in frantic attempts to escape any form of containment.

Wild Rose: A good choice for dogs who are so unable to deal with a situation that they become totally "shut down." These are the dogs who will not eat when the owner is away, and may withdraw into themselves. Dogs who have been abandoned often display a sort of learned helplessness, and fall into this category as well.

You may have noticed there is a bit of overlap in these descriptions. But while Honeysuckle and Heather, for example, may be useful for some of the same issues, one essence may work much more effectively for a particular individual. Try one essence at a time to gauge its value, or, if time is pressing, use them in combination.

Making a Combination Bottle

You can combine up to six essences, but using fewer is fine, too. Rescue® Remedy can be used in combination with individual essences. It will not interfere with their healing effects, and will work synergistically to reinforce them. If you use Rescue® Remedy, since it already contains five essences, count it as five rather than one.

Suppose you adopted a dog from the shelter, and his paperwork said only that he had been abandoned. He is now having trouble adjusting to life in your home. He is afraid to let you out of his sight, and whenever you leave him alone, he becomes absolutely frantic to the point that you are afraid he might injure himself. You decide that Star of Bethlehem, Walnut, Chicory, and Rock Rose would be the perfect combination to help with those issues.

The next step is to make a combination bottle. Dark glass bottles are sold for this purpose at health food stores and other retailers that carry flower essences. The bottles normally hold 30 ml of fluid, but a 10 ml bottle is fine, too. Fill the clean, empty dropper bottle three quarters of the way with spring water. Add two to three drops of each remedy, and then shake to mix the contents. When stored in the refrigerator, the mixture should last approximately five days.

You can also purchase pre-made combinations of flower essences that are designed to address specific emotional problems. A few companies that carry combinations formulated for separation issues are listed in the *Resources* section.

Administration of Essences

Whether you are using an individual essence, Rescue® Remedy, or a combination you created, the liquid may be administered in a variety of ways. The most popular method is to add four drops to your dog's drinking water four times daily. If he doesn't tend to drink much water, you can place the drops directly into your dog's mouth between the lip and gum, but take care that he doesn't touch the glass dropper, or worse, bite down on it. As a last resort, the drops can be placed on your dog's food. If your dog eats twice daily, eight drops with each meal is fine.

Essences may also be diluted with water and sprayed around your dog or the environment, rubbed into your dog's gums (but not directly from the dropper!), or fed on a small piece of bread. Rescue® Remedy also comes in a spray form which can be used in much the same way as the D.A.P. spray products.

Frequent dosage is key. There is no need for concern regarding overdosing—there is no chance of a dog overdosing on flower essences, although the alcohol base could cause a problem if enormous amounts were administered at once. (Rescue® Remedy is now available in a glycerin base, which negates any potential alcohol problems.) It is said that if a dog does not need a particular essence, no change will take place. If an essence does help, the effects are usually fairly subtle. In other words, your dog may become calmer, but he will not look dazed or appear as though he has been given a tranquilizer.

Although there has not been much scientific study on the efficacy of flower essences, I include them here because there is anecdotal evidence of their usefulness for animals and people. Like everything else, flower essences may or may not work for your dog. But because they are safe to use alone or in conjunction with other treatments, and are inexpensive and widely available, they are certainly worth trying.

If you have questions about flower essences or would like more individualized help, The Flower Essence Society (see *Resources*) can answer questions and refer you to a practitioner in your area.

17

Body Wraps

Why, you might wonder, would you want to wrap your dog up like a beagle burrito or a Chihuahua enchilada? Well, if you've ever seen an infant swaddled in a blanket, you might have noticed that the baby was calm and quiet. The uniform pressure created by close-fitting, comfortable material is very soothing to babies. The concept has also been applied to help autistic children, and even non-autistic kids with certain types of behavioral problems.

Animals too can be made less nervous through the use of pressurized restraint. Cows, for example, feel less anxious being led to slaughter when they are placed in a well-designed squeeze chute. Temple Grandin, author, animal activist, and pioneer of the chute, discusses in her books how she, as an autistic child, designed a "hug box" that made her feel more secure. Being swaddled, gently squeezed, or snugly wrapped in an appropriate fabric creates uniform pressure, which in turn creates a relaxation response.

Body wraps, or pressure wraps as they are sometimes called, can help dogs to feel more relaxed and secure in a variety of situations. They can be used in the treatment of a variety of fears and phobias, including those where the triggers are loud noises, having nails trimmed, riding in cars, being around other dogs—and being left alone.

T-Shirt Wrap

There are different types and brands of body wraps available for purchase, as well as a few kinds you can create yourself. The easiest do-it-yourself version is the T-shirt wrap. Choose a T-shirt meant for a human child or adult that is appropriately sized for your dog, and use slow, gentle movements to place it on him. Position the shirt upside down—if there is a logo on the front, it should end up on your dog's back—as it will fit more closely that way. Once you've got your dog's arms through the armholes, gather the material by pulling both sides up toward the back. The resulting fit should be snug, but not so tight that it restricts movement or cuts off circulation. Secure the shirt with a large rubber band. Take care not to place the knot directly over your dog's spine, as that could cause discomfort.

If your dog has not worn "clothing" before, you may have to take some time to desensitize him to it before use. You might start by pulling the neck hole over his head, offering a treat or two, then immediately removing the shirt. (If even that is too much, start by simply touching the shirt to his chest and feeding a treat, then, as long as he remains relaxed, touch the shirt to his head, treat, and progress incrementally from there.) After a few repetitions, as long as your dog still seems comfortable, pull the shirt over his head and gently maneuver a paw through a sleeve. Give a few treats in rapid succession, and then remove the shirt. Take your time and keep the mood light. Continue in this manner until your dog is comfortable having the shirt put on and removed.

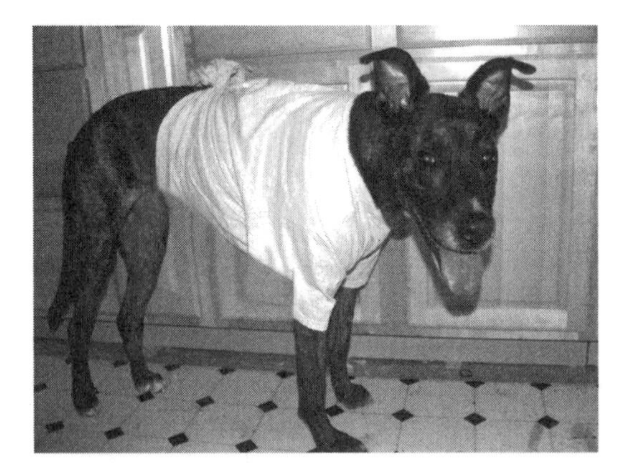

As an alternative to using a T-shirt, you could instead use a lightweight sweater or other item of "dog clothing," as it will already be the correct size. Just be sure the material creates a snug enough fit for the purpose.

Prefabricated Wraps

There are a few different brands of prefabricated canine body wraps. The one I prefer is the Thundershirt™. Made of soft, lightweight material, the product hugs the body comfortably and is easy to use, thanks to the clever design and Velcro closures. Placing it on a dog does not entail pulling anything over the head, which is the part to which many dogs object. I've been able to place Thundershirts on uninitiated dogs in under thirty seconds, and I've yet to encounter a dog who objected to wearing one. (Of course, any dog with serious issues about being handled will need desensitization first, regardless of which product you use.)

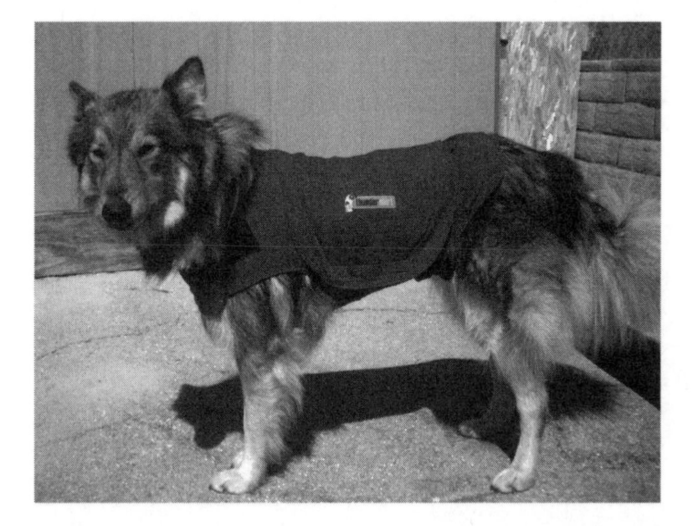

Accustom your dog to wearing the wrap when you are at home by associating it with things he likes. Place the wrap on him, let him wear it while he eats a meal, and remove it right afterward. Or put it on, offer a few treats, and then remove it. If your dog enjoys walks, allow him to wear the wrap while out on a fun stroll. You get the idea.

How to Use the Wrap

Once your dog has become conditioned to the wrap, place it on him a few minutes before you begin to work on in-home separation protocols such as building distance or staying out of sight. You can also use the wrap when you're practicing more informal separations, such as having your dog relax, perhaps with a chew item, in his crate, on a bed, behind a gate, or whenever there is a bit of physical separation involved. The uniform pressure will help to calm your dog and allow him to settle. Remove the wrap a few minutes after the session is over.

Note that using the wrap when you are at home to supervise should not be confused with putting the wrap on your dog and then leaving the house. It is not recommended to leave dogs unattended when wearing any type of body wrap.

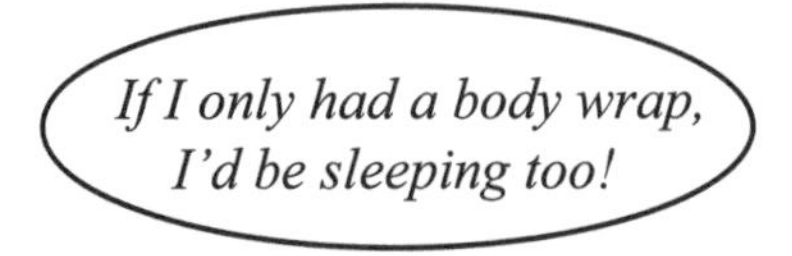

PART V

The Light at the End of the Tunnel

Putting it All Together

You should now have a better idea of how to address your dog's separation issues. Perhaps you've already made some changes, such as improving his diet or increasing his daily exercise. Maybe you've begun to look into some of the recommended adjunctive therapies. Great! Now for the final step: constructing your overall plan. Having a cohesive strategy you can hold in your hand will bolster your confidence that your dog's issues are manageable and ultimately solvable. It will also help to keep you and your family members on track, and will provide a concrete way to gauge your progress.

Throughout this book, you have been asked to provide responses to questions on topics such as management, departure cues, graduated absences, and more. Now it's time to put it all together. The Format Guide below explains each component of the treatment plan. A Sample Plan follows, and finally, a Treatment Plan for you to fill out for *your* dog.

Format Guide

Description: A brief overview of the issue and your dog's behavior when you are away.

Management: A complete list of available options to help avoid leaving your dog alone during the course of the behavior modification period.

Exercise and Recreational Chewing/Mental Stimulation: What type of physical exercise your dog will receive, how often, and who will provide it. Include recreational chewing and mental stimulation (for example, specific chew items or treat dispensing interactive toys).

Nutrition: What type and brand of food your dog is currently eating and, if you plan to change it, a description of the new diet.

Training: List the skills your dog already knows, any new skills you plan to teach, and who will practice with your dog. Note too whether you plan to work with a professional trainer on the separation issue and/or basic obedience skills.

The Plan: Based on what you have read and the notes you have made so far, formulate an overall behavior modification plan. The protocol may be broken down into phases. Include a brief description of what you will be doing at each step. Note that this is an overview of the entire plan, not just the behavioral training you plan to implement immediately.

Adjunctive Therapies: State whether you will try any of the supplements or tools mentioned in the Cool Tools section, and if so, which ones.

Below is a sample plan that features the Sklar family and Buddy, their year-old German Shepherd mix. Husband Dan works Monday through Friday outside of the home. Wife Lisa does not work, but has standing social engagements a few days each week. Teens Jennifer and Justin attend school Monday through Friday from 9:00 a.m. to 3:00 p.m., and are otherwise at home or out with their friends. Buddy is the family's only pet. The plan that follows is written from Lisa's point of view.

Sample Treatment Plan for Buddy

Description: Buddy is a great dog, but he gets very upset when we leave him alone. We left the camcorder running for an hour when we were gone, and learned that Buddy barks non-stop, grabs things off the coffee table and countertops and eats or destroys them, and seems very agitated and unable to settle down the whole time we're away. Also, when we come home, he does that over-the-top frantic greeting, jumping and pawing at us, even wrapping his arms around our legs so we won't walk away.

Management: On the weekends a few of us are usually at home. But whether it's a weekend or a weekday, if it turns out only one of us is at home and has to go out for a little while, we can take Buddy with us. On Tuesday and Thursday mornings when I go to the gym, I can drop Buddy off at neighbor Michelle's house, since he gets along well with their dog Dancer. (This could also work if I have to do errands and it's too hot out to leave Buddy in the car.) If Michelle is going out, we'll ask her to drop Dancer off here, and the dogs can stay out in the yard. Sometimes we can bring Buddy to the Oh My Dog! daycare center.

For at-home management, we'll use the kitchen with a tall baby gate across the entrance. This will be Buddy's Alone Zone when we practice departures. If there's an emergency and we absolutely have to leave him alone at home, we'll use a different spot so we don't "contaminate" the progress we've been making in the Alone Zone.

Exercise and Recreational Chewing/Mental Stimulation: Every weekday, Justin takes Buddy for a half-hour walk in the morning before school, and Jennifer takes him for a forty-five minute to an hour walk when she gets home. On the weekends we take him to the park or for a hike. We will make sure he keeps getting at least an hour of exercise each day, and will try to arrange some play dates so he can burn off even more energy. We are also looking for a local agility class, since Buddy loves to jump up on things and seems very agile! It would be great to help him spend some of that energy while building confidence.

We will continue to give Buddy bully sticks to chew on, since he really enjoys them and they take him a while to finish. I will buy a Kong toy and we will all experiment with different ways to stuff it, and sometimes freeze it. Maybe we'll even have a contest! Jennifer and I will look into other treat-dispensing toys online as well.

Nutrition: After reading the ingredients in Buddy's dry food we've decided to change to a better brand. I will do some research at the local pet food store and online. We'll switch him over gradually so he doesn't get tummy upset.

Training: We've been working on short obedience training sessions throughout the day, and the kids have learned from a DVD to teach Buddy tricks like shake and roll over. We use his favorite treats, and he really enjoys the training. We are all having him practice down-stays behind the kitchen baby gate, and our immediate goal is to have him down-stay with us out of sight so he feels calm hanging out in the kitchen alone.

The Plan: Because Buddy follows whoever is home all over the house and doesn't want to let them out of his sight, we will practice separations with him behind the baby gate. We will experiment to see how he does with the down-stays there and will also do the suggested protocol where he's left with scattered treats for short periods, building to longer ones. We will gradually increase the distance, and then in the next phase, start with very short out of sight visual separations, again increasing the time bit by bit. We'll make sure that in some of the visual separation practice, we move toward the front door.

In the meantime, we are teaching Buddy to "settle" so we can use it around the house for casual separations each day.

We are desensitizing Buddy to departure cues. We have each made a list of what our cues are. Mine normally include filling his water dish, putting on my shoes, putting on my jacket, grabbing my cell phone from the charger and putting it in my purse, picking up my purse, picking up my keys, and walking out the door. We'll each try to do a few of our cues a few times a day, and vary the order during practice and in our real departure routines.

Once Buddy stops being nervous when we're getting ready to leave and is okay with short out of sight separations behind the baby gate, we'll begin to work on walking out the front door and coming right back, then staying outside the door for longer periods, walking out to the car, starting it up, and so forth—baby steps. Eventually, we will start doing real departures, short ones at first and then building up. If at any point the whole thing gets too overwhelming or we don't think we're making enough progress, I will look into hiring a behavior specialist.

Adjunctive Tools: I am getting Buddy used to the body wrap and plan to use it during settles and during the protocols. He doesn't seem to mind it at all. We are playing soft classical music for short periods and will eventually let it play when he's left alone. Sometimes one of us massages him or pets him while the music is on, and we make a point of having it on both when he's in his Alone Zone and at other times.

Treatment Plan for ______________________

Description: ______________________

Management: ______________________

Exercise and Recreational Chewing/Mental Stimulation: ________

Nutrition: ______________________

Training: ______________________

The Plan: ______________________

Adjunctive Tools: ______________________

Once you've designed a customized plan to help your dog feel calm and secure when left alone, you're ready to begin. Keep a progress log. This doesn't need to be a time-consuming activity. Just make a quick note each day as to what you worked on, and the results. Below is a sample entry for Buddy, once he is at the point where the family can leave him alone in the house for brief periods.

1/20 Dan is at work and the kids are at school. I had to go to the market. I gave Buddy a bully stick and left five minutes later. He was lying in the kitchen behind the gate chewing when I left. He looked up for a second or two but went right back to chewing. He seemed calm when I came home 20 minutes later, and the greeting was happy but not frantic. Hurray!

Set up the camcorder periodically so you have a realistic idea of your dog's activities when you're gone. Between the recordings and the log entries, you'll soon be able to see just how much progress you've made.

~ * ~ * ~ * ~ * ~ * ~ * ~ * ~ * ~ * ~ * ~

Remember that the results you can expect to achieve depend on a combination of your dog's genetic "blueprint," his life experience, and your efforts. Some dogs who are genetically predisposed to being anxious may never feel *completely* relaxed when left alone—but even those dogs can make significant progress. For example, a dog who was originally pacing and barking non-stop might now instead do a bit of pacing and barking, then go and lie down to keep watch for your return. For many dogs, however, it is absolutely realistic to expect that they will eventually feel calm enough when left home alone to relax and even to take naps.

I urge you to take advantage of the *Resources* section that follows, as it is a useful compilation of organizations, informational sources, and recommended products. The more you know, and the more tools at your disposal, the better equipped you will be to help your dog.

My heart and hopes go out to you as you and your dog undertake this journey together. Be patient, be compassionate, and know that there *is* a light at the end of the tunnel. My highest hope is that you and your dog will soon be feeling much more relaxed, and that this book will become but a fond memory.

Sierra's Story Nicole Wilde, CPDT-KA

Although I have shared bits and pieces of Sierra's journey throughout the book, my hope is that by reading the full account, complete with its challenges and difficulties, you will be encouraged to follow through in working with your own dog's separation issues.

The winter of 2008 was a bleak one for my husband and me. We'd lost our last remaining senior dogs including Mojo, who was like a child to us. Grief and an endless deafening silence filled the house. But time heals, and a year later the search for a new dog began.

After a few months of diligent searching online and at local shelters and humane societies, I found a year-old Husky-Keeshond mix at an overcrowded county shelter in the desert. She'd been picked up as a stray, and since no one had appeared to claim her, my husband and I arrived on the "available" date to bail her out. That's when we found out this had been her fourth time in the shelter! The staff could not provide us with more information. Undaunted, we took her home.

From the beginning, Sierra was a sweet soul: gentle, affectionate, and, happily for us, completely non-destructive. But we soon noticed that whenever we returned from an outing without her, she was panting, wide-eyed, and frantic to greet us. I set up a video camera so I could find out what she was doing while we were away.

It was worse than I'd thought, and reviewing the footage was a painful experience. Sierra paced from the front door to the French doors, back and forth, whimpering. The whimpering turned into an intense whining, which escalated into barking. Next came a frantic barking, and finally, a mournful howl that I could hardly bear. Her distress continued for the entire forty-five minutes. This was a serious separation issue. That it existed wasn't surprising, given what we knew of her history, but the intensity of her behavior was stronger than I'd expected.

Strangely, some people couldn't understand why I thought there was a problem. Sierra didn't destroy things, she didn't urinate or defecate in the house, and even with the vocalizing, my nearest neighbors were far enough away that no one would complain. But my dog was in distress! That stress would eventually take a toll on her health, and besides, it was just *not okay* for her to suffer that way.

I immediately implemented a strict management program. If I had errands to run, Sierra came along. If I absolutely needed to go someplace I couldn't take her, my husband arranged to come home from work a bit early, or to go in a bit late. I explained to friends why I was turning down invitations to lunch and other social engagements. My husband and I both made many sacrifices. In addition, I refrained from doing what I really wanted to do, which involved constantly cuddling that adorable fur face to within an inch of her life!

At the same time, I began a behavior modification program. Sierra's case is atypical, in that she did not follow us around the house or act clingy. She loved to be outdoors, and would lie on the ramp just outside the dog door for hours, content as long as she knew someone was in the house. Because I knew she was happiest outdoors, and was non-destructive indoors, I elected to leave her loose with the dog door open rather than conditioning her to being in an Alone Zone. I did, however, desensitize her to the few departure cues that would inevitably cause her to come running inside whenever she heard them. I mixed up the order of the cues regularly as well.

Part of our challenge was that Sierra was not only sensitive, but was also somewhat shut down when she first came to us. When training a stay, I had put my palm up in a small, mild gesture. Sierra's ears went back, her eyes narrowed, and she looked for all the world as though she was afraid I was going to hit her. Training was a challenge, as she consistently demonstrated learned helplessness—she was afraid to try anything for fear of being wrong. I sadly wondered what sort of punishment she had suffered in the past.

Another manifestation of Sierra's being shut down was her lack of interest in unstuffing a Kong, rolling around a ball with treats in it, or attempting anything that was at all challenging. I tried to leave her with bully sticks and other simple chew items, but she wasn't interested. After trying a variety of things, I finally discovered that Frosty Paws (ice cream for dogs) was tantalizing enough and easy enough to lick from its little paper cup that she'd eat it when we were gone. Another successful solution was to smear peanut butter on a bully stick or other item, where it was easy to get to.

I practiced a classic departure protocol each day, building up over a few weeks to being able to drive down the road, sit for a few minutes, and then drive back up the driveway. These multiple daily departures were particularly challenging because we were experiencing southern California's rainy season, which, believe it or not, can get quite stormy! As you might imagine, going out in the rain and cold multiple times daily was not my idea of fun. During this period, I also practiced short, easy training sessions to build Sierra's confidence. She gradually began to lose the learned helplessness, and became interested in and even enjoyed training. Her "take a bow" trick made me smile from ear to ear.

We had been adamant from the beginning that Sierra would have plenty of exercise. Each day she'd get roughly an hour and a half of physical exertion, whether by playing with a canine friend at the dog park (early, before others arrived), hiking with my husband, pulling a scooter (urban mushing), or some other fun activity. I strongly believe that providing plenty of exercise has been largely responsible for the success of the graduated departures. To this day, we make sure that if we're going to see a movie or planning another type of outing, Sierra is well tired out beforehand.

As to the "Cool Tools" mentioned in this book, I have to admit that as much as they have helped countless dogs belonging to my clients, none made an iota of difference with Sierra. *Hmm*, I thought as one after the other failed, *I guess this is the Universe's way of making sure I stay humble!* It was frustrating, but there *was* progress in various areas. Things improved little by little.

I was soon able to get Sierra chewing on a bully stick and licking peanut butter that I'd stuffed in a hollow, sterilized bone. If I made the Kong super easy to excavate, she was willing to try.

The practice departures eventually lengthened to where I could leave Sierra alone for longer and longer periods. Strangely, she seemed to have an internal timer that was set for ninety minutes. Any absence over that time, and she'd become anxious. By that point I'd been diligently working on the issue for about seven weeks. Although that might not sound like a long time, when you're intimately involved with the problem on a daily basis, it can seem like forever. You may remember that this was the point at which I decided that one of us had to be on drugs. I consulted my veterinarian, and we started Sierra on clomipramine. Five days in, she noticeably relaxed. I continued the behavior modification protocol, and Sierra continued to improve.

As I write this, it is exactly seven months from the day we brought Sierra home. I won't say she's completely "cured," but for a dog who's been through so much in her short life, it's a major improvement. She is still on Zylkene, and I am in the process of weaning her off the clomipramine. We may at some point adopt a boy toy—er, companion—for Sierra. This could solve her issue completely, as she has isolation distress, not separation from a particular person; then again, it might not. Either way, having a buddy would most likely make her happier, and would give her another outlet for that mega-playful energy.

Sierra is finally at the point where she can remain relaxed for a few hours while we are gone. We still wouldn't leave her alone for a full day, and we can all live with that. Our twentieth wedding anniversary is coming up, and rather than boarding Sierra in a kennel while we fly off to some exotic destination, we're going to drive up to a woodsy resort area and rent a cabin that allows dogs. It should be fun.

The day we adopted Sierra from the shelter I told the clerk, "Say goodbye, because you'll never see this dog again." I meant it. Sierra has a forever home, and we feel very lucky to have found her.

Sierra

Resources

Flower Essences

Bach Flower Remedies for Animals
Helen Graham and Gregory Vlamis
Tallahassee, FL: Findhorn Press, 1999 ISBN 1-899171-72-X

Bach Flower Remedies for Dogs
Martin J. Scott and Gael Mariani
Scotland: Findhorn Press, 2007 ISBN 978-1-84409-099-0

Bach Flower Remedies are available through www.bachflower.com and a number of other online retailers.

Five Flower Formula – Flower Essence Services (FES)
http://www.fesflowers.com

The Flower Essence Society
http://www.flowersociety.org

Interactive Toys

Atomic Treat Ball
Available through pet supply stores, amazon.com, and other online retailers.

Kong interactive toys and Kong stuffing recipes
www.kongcompany.com

MannersMinder
www.premier.com

Nina Ottosson products
www.nina-ottosson.com

Videos of Sierra testing interactive toys:

Aikiou Interactive Food Bowl
http://bit.ly/bbDXrE

Kong Wobbler
http://bit.ly/9dZQnr

Nina Ottoson toys and others
http://bit.ly/8Xz0kO

Nutrition

The BARF Diet: Raw Feeding for Dogs and Cats using Evolutionary Principles
Ian Billinghurst
Australia: Billinghurst, 2001 ISBN 978-0958592512

Unlocking the Canine Ancestral Diet
Steve Brown
Wenatchee, WA: Dogwise Publishing, 2009 ISBN 978-1929242672

Foods Pets Die For: Shocking Facts About Pet Food
Ann N. Martin
Troutdale, OR: NewSage Press, 2003 ISBN 0939165465

Dr. Pitcairn's New Complete Guide to Natural Health for Dogs & Cats
Richard H. Pitcairn, DVM, Ph.D. & Susan Hubble Pitcairn
Emmaus, PA: Rodale Press, Inc. 2005 ISBN 978-1579549732

Natural Nutrition for Dogs and Cats
Kymythy R. Schultze
Carlsbad, CA: Hay House, Inc., 1999 ISBN 978-1561706365

The Dog Food Project website
www.dogfoodproject.com

Pet Friendly Places, Pet Sitters

DogFriendly.com's United States and Canada Dog Travel Guide
Dogfriendly.com, 2010 ISBN 978-0979555107
www.dogfriendly.com

Pet Sitters International
http://www.petsit.com/owners (click on "Locate a pet sitter")

Products

Bicycle attachments
K9 cruiser: www.k9cruiser.com
Springer Bicycle Jogger: online retailers, find via search engine

D.A.P.
Sold as D.A.P. or Comfort Zone via retailers,
and through your veterinarian.

Gates
In the Company of Dogs offer a variety of sizes and configurations.
www.inthecompanyofdogs.com
Also, enter "dog gates" at any online search engine.

Tethers
www.raisewithpraise.com, www.baddogsinc.com

Through a Dog's Ear
Volume 1 of the series is carried by Phantom Publishing (www.phantompub.com). The entire product line is also available directly from Through a Dog's Ear at www.throughadogsear.com.

Thundershirt
Phantom Publishing: www.phantompub.com
and www.thundershirt.com

Sports

Agility
Competition: NADAC (www.nadac.com)
& USDAA (www.usdaa.com)
General information: http://en.wikipedia.org/wiki/Dog_agility

Canine Freestyle
WCFO: www.worldcaninefreestyle.org
Canine Freestyle Federation: www.canine-freestyle.org
Musical Dog Sport Association: www.musicaldogsport.org

K9 Nosework
www.k9nosework.com

Rally
AKC: www.akc.org/events/rally
APDT: www.apdt.com/rally

Urban Mushing
www.urbanmushing.com

Training and Behavior

Books

Dogwise (www.dogwise.com) carries these and other excellent titles.

Dog-Friendly Dog Training
Andrea Arden
New York, NY: Howell Books, 1999 ISBN 1-582450099

How to Teach an Old Dog New Tricks
Dr. Ian Dunbar
UK: James & Kenneth, 1998 ISBN 978-1888047066

The Power of Positive Dog Training
Pat Miller
New York, NY: Hungry Minds, Inc., 2001 ISBN 0-7645-3609-5

The Dog Whisperer: A Compassionate, Non-Violent Approach to Dog Training
Paul Owens
Hollbrook, MA: Adams Media Corp., 2006 ISBN

Help for Your Fearful Dog
Nicole Wilde
Santa Clarita, CA: Phantom Publishing, 2006 ISBN 0-9667726-7-9
www.phantompub.com

DVDs

Train Your Dog: The Positive, Gentle Method
The Picture Company, Inc., 2003 UPC 829637 12237 0
www.phantompub.com and www.trainyourdog.tv

The How of Bow Wow (obedience) and Take a Bow I & II (tricks)
Virginia Broitman & Sherri Lipman
www.takeabowwow.com

Tawzer Dog Videos (offers a variety of excellent training DVDs)
www.tawzerdogvideos.com

Trainers and Behavior Specialists

Association of Pet Dog Trainers (APDT)
1-800-PET-DOGS
www.apdt.com

Veterinary Behaviorists
www.veterinarybehaviorists.org

American Veterinary Society of Animal Behaviorists (AVSAB)
http://bit.ly/9t0JF2

Miscellaneous

Merck Veterinary Manual
http://www.merckvetmanual.com

Books, DVDs and Seminars
by Nicole Wilde
HELP FOR YOUR
FEARFUL DOG
A Step-by-Step Guide to Helping
Your Dog Conquer His Fears
Nicole
Wilde,
CPDT
"Easy to follow, often humorous, and incredibly helpful!
A MUST-READ for any owner or trainer of fearful dogs."
So You Want to be a
Dog Trainer
A Step-by-Step Guide
2nd edition
Nicole Wilde, CPDT
the POSITIVE GENTLE method
train
your
DOG
WORKING WITH
FEARFUL DOGS
Seminar Video
A Step-by-Step Guide to Helping
Your Dog Conquer His Fears
Nicole
Wilde,
CPDT
For more titles, products, excerpts, and
reviews, visit Phantom Publishing
www.phantompub.com